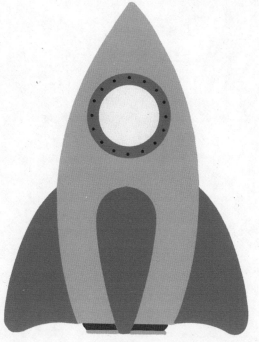

Krista!

I am so glad
we connected!
I hope we can
do. lets get
together!

B.

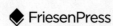

FriesenPress

Suite 300 - 990 Fort St
Victoria, BC, V8V 3K2
Canada

www.friesenpress.com

Copyright © 2017 by Brian Hogben
First Edition — 2017

ISBN
978-1-5255-1183-7 (Hardcover)
978-1-5255-1184-4 (Paperback)
978-1-5255-1185-1 (eBook)

1. BUSINESS & ECONOMICS, PERSONAL FINANCE, MONEY MANAGEMENT

Distributed to the trade by The Ingram Book Company

MISSION35

Your first step in Financial Security

Brian Hogben

When I was twenty-five years old, my dad loaned me $5,000 to purchase my first rental property. He said, "Brian, I will loan you the money because I believe in you, but I don't understand. Why do you need two houses? You can only live in one at a time!"

He was the first person to believe in me (and you must understand that I wanted to make a lot of money and try and retire at the age of thirty-five). He never really understood my passion, but he always gave his total support. He would even stay up late after his own workday and help me paint one of my rental properties until the wee hours of the morning.

When my dad suddenly passed away from leukemia, I was inspired to write this book, as he was the best man I've ever known. His attitude on life, his commitment to his family, and his knowledge of money gave my brother and I a childhood most people could only dream of. We were not wealthy by any means; I only remember eating out twice as a child, once at the Olive Garden, and the other at Swiss Chalet—and those were *very* special occasions!

Even though my dad's financial education was different from mine, he was an inspiration to me. He used to say that if he were born in a different time, he would have been a millionaire, and things would have been very different for my brother and I—but he only knew what his parents told him. My father had a factory job at a steel mill in Hamilton, and he spent the better part of his days working there. He retired at the age of fifty-nine. After almost forty years at a job where they had "guaranteed" him a pension, this was the best option that he knew of in order to provide a life for himself and his family. The "security" of having benefits and a pension made him feel good about what he was doing; however, I believe it also robbed him of trying something different. He loved numbers, so maybe he could have been an accountant. He also loved coaching, maybe he could have gone on to be a professional basketball coach after getting my brother and I through the house league teams.

Pops would do all of our family's taxes, and he'd even do some for the neighbours, for fun and for *free* (it takes a special type of person to *want* to do taxes in the first place, and an even more special person to not even charge people for it). He learned all of it all on his own, and he used to fill them all out by hand with his pencil, calculator, and a pack of cigarettes on the kitchen table. He would get so excited and take so much pride in saving people money. "You know, if you put some money into a spousal RRSP before the deadline, you guys could get some additional money back," he would tell the neighbours. Every single penny he could save for someone made him so happy.

I remember telling him once, "You should do this for a living. People could pay you to do this—and you actually love doing it!"

My dad was the type of guy who made the best of every situation. I don't think he hated his job, but I am quite sure it didn't give him the joy that doing taxes and saving money for people did. "I can't leave my job," he'd reply. "I only have seven years, 3 months, and 5 days left till retirement." He always knew—down to the hour—when he could escape the rat race and be done. That retirement, and the "promise" of a pension, fuelled him though a long time at that place.

As some of you probably know (and have lived through), the shitty part about it all is that companies with "guaranteed pensions" are absolutely *not* guaranteed. When my dad was passing, the company went into receivership, and eventually into bankruptcy, and then the pensioners, such as my dad, were robbed of the privileges they had been promised for years. Benefits? Gone! Security in retirement? Gone! Providing for your spouse after death? Gone! Now, my dad was smart; as when he was in his younger years he paid off his house as fast as he could. He actually had it paid off in only 9 years, that was his and my moms top priority as soon as they moved in. They sacrificed going out to eat, for BBQs at home, lavish vacations, for fun times at there home with friends. Having no mortgage and being in a strong financial position helped when he got the terrible news, at least it was one less thing to worry about. He had saved money along the way too, so even without his pension, he would still be able to provide for my mom, but his lifestyle would have to change. With no pension, to be honest it would probably keep him in the same lifestyle that he had as they were not big spenders, but it would have created more stress and made him restrict his spending even more. The mental stress of losing his pension would have been greater then any financial hardship it would put on him. After he passed, my mom was still in a good situation. She had more than enough money to live a comfortable life. No matter how hard she tried she could not waste money, even on a spending spree it would be at a dollar store or thrift shop

This entire situation with the loss of my dad's pension made me so angry. I swore to myself that I would never leave my financial security up to someone else, as the idea that someone (like a business or even the government) will take care of you is bullshit. I live in Canada, and I am "supposed" to get a small pension from the government at the age of sixty or sixty-five, but what if they decide to stop paying it twenty years from now? What am I going to do—protest, or start a riot? The only guarantee is that there is nothing I could do to get my money if that was the case. The reality with Canada Pension and Old Age Security is that it was designed when the life expectancy was sixty-five! People are living well into their eighties and longer now, think about this. It means that more people are actually drawing on Canada Pension Plans and Old Age Security, than there are people that pay into these same pensions. Not to mention the massive increase in people that are self employed who may not necessarily declare all of there cash money. This creates an even bigger drag on our National pensions which many people believe will be there for them later in life. I do hope that it is there for myself and the generations to come, but I won't bet on it, and if it is, then *great*—I will happily take that money. My mission has always been to ensure that me and my family's financial health is in order, and that it's not left up to someone else to ensure that we will be okay. Someone else is not going to tell me, "Your money is doing just fine," and someone else is not going to tell me, "There was a market correction." Someone else is not going to be delivering my family any bad news of "Well, you should have, could have, would have."

Mission 35 is a vision. It is about taking your finances into your own hands and being responsible for them. Mission 35 is about creating security in your life and not letting your finances rule your life. In this book you will learn how to make money, how to save money, and how to invest it, and you won't leave your financial health in the hands of someone who "has your best interests at heart." Someone can truly only have your best interests at heart if all of *their* interests are covered first. In *most* cases, wherever you are investing your money, they are looking at their own benefit first—not yours. Having been in the banking industry for most of my life, I know that finances scare most people, and a lot of people just don't like arriving at the reality that the current situation may not be as rosy as they think. It is important to know where you are in order to know where you are going. My mission is to share with people how an ordinary guy from a blue-collar family did it—which in my eyes, means that anyone reading this can do it, as well.

$1.85 million: is that a big number? To some it may be huge, and to others it may be small. To me, it is a very significant number. What that number represents is fifteen years of choices—choices that allowed me to say, "Freedom 35!" on my thirty-fifth birthday. Freedom 35 or Mission 35 is about being free from living in a mind-space of being stuck. In the olden days that would be retirement, where you can leave a job you hate or stop doing things you have to do for money and never work again! I would like to redefine retirement, as achieving financial security. In my Mission, financial security doesn't necessarily mean not working and doing nothing all day, but what it does mean to me is *choosing* to do exactly what you want to do, when you want to do it. It means choosing your lifestyle, your house, your business, or whatever it may be that fits with your passions, goals and dreams. It means not being stuck in a situation where you "HAVE TO" go to work to pay the bills. It means having the freedom to say, "If I sell it all today, I can live happily forever for the rest of my life!"

You may be thinking, *That's impossible. How can you live off of $1.85 million for the rest of your life?* Well, that comes with the idea that you choose the lifestyle you want to live. I know I can live in a house with a value of $400,000. I choose not to today, but would be comfortable as a pig in you know what if I had to downsized into a nice 3 bedroom bungalow in order to pursue my dreams. That would completely suit my needs. With the balance of my funds I could invest it at a yield of 10% per annum, quite easily which would give me the income that I require in order to take care of my family for a life time. 10%? You may be asking? Keep reading and you will see how that comes into play, you will learn that type of rate is not unrealistic. This is how I can comfortably say, "Freedom 35." The freedom is having the security to choose what do I want to do next. This Mission requires some skills, some money, and even more knowledge. I have learned how to choose a lifestyle on a $100,000 income that includes vacations to places like Ireland, Las Vegas, San Francisco, Jamaica, Puerto Vallarta, the Bahamas, and my favourite, St. Barths! In this book, I will talk to you a lot about choices, but sacrificing things on the vacation side was one budgeting strategy that wasn't for me. What did I sacrifice on? My house today is worth over a million dollars and it is paid for, *but* that does not mean that it does not have debt against it. You need to know the difference between good debt and bad debt. In my neighbourhood, I live beside two doctors with a third doctor three houses down, so it's a pretty swanky area in my neck of the woods. However, I drove a 2009 Ford Escape for the past five years, which was worth no more than $8,000 when I traded it in after my thirty-fifth birthday for my new 2015 Jeep Cherokee Overland.

The car was my one big sacrifice. The other one—and the biggest one—was my time. I sacrificed a lot of time from my early twenties to my early thirties. A lot of friends asked me where I was when I was working twelve hours a day building my career, and then going to paint one of my rental properties until 2:00 a.m. because a new tenant was moving in. Then I'd go back to work again at 8:00 a.m. People would say, "Your life is passing you by," and to them I'd say, "Bullshit! I would rather work hard for ten years and live the next fifty doing exactly what I want to do, instead of living sixty years in my working career feeling like I am tolerating a life in which I know I deserve better."

The Freedom Journey means doing the things today that people aren't willing to, in order to do the things tomorrow that other people can't do. The journey is about sacrificing some big ticket items, such as where you live, what you drive, or where you vacation. As we live in a debt driven society it is easy to get most things you want today through credit. By delaying some of these purchases and using the funds for investment instead of consumption your wealth grows exceeding faster the sooner you start this process. It is by no means an easy one, but when your life opens up to you at the age of thirty-five, I have a hard time even putting into the words the euphoria that will come over you. The choices, options, confidence, and opportunities that come your way because of what you have accomplished start to become endless.

I want to communicate to you—especially the younger generations out there, from teenagers to kids in their early-to-late twenties and even early thirties—that making some *big* choices and *big* goals when you are younger can have *big* wins for you before you know it. I have outlined in the coming pages the major life decisions and key drivers that helped me to get to where I am today. I am going to outline why these things are important, and I'll provide the valuable, real-life experiences that I had to go through in order to not only learn the lesson, but to reach the destination. Mission35 was my mission, and it was my goal. Your Mission can be Mission25 or Mission65 or anywhere in between. I believe that the sooner you set a target in mind the sooner you will be able to track your progress and get hustling on your plan.

In the eleven chapters, I have broken down my experiences into what I think is most valuable. In each chapter you will find three sections:

1. **"What Happened"** includes my life experiences. This means the good, the bad, and the ugly, no holds barred.

2. **"What I Made It Mean"** is key, as in all of our experiences, we have the ability to decide on the meaning that we take out of them. Your interpretation of your life experiences will be crucial to the overall Mission.

3. **"What To Do"** offers the action plans you can take from all of my mistakes (and believe me, there were a lot) to help you streamline your Mission objective.

Below is a summary of the chapters, each one focused on a different step to your success.

Chapter 1: Goals

I am sure you have heard it a million times before: "What's your goal? Blah, blah, blah." This has always been—and will always be—a big part of my life. Setting goals helps you to know where you are going, and how to get there. Not having any goals in your life is like throwing darts at a wall and then painting the target around it, saying to yourself, "Yup, that's where I was aiming for." Bullshit! Set your goals. In this section you will learn how to set your FIA number. This is your "Forget it All" Number. This is your financial security number. This is the goal. This is the starting point, the back bone, and the key to your Mission.

Chapter 2: Mentors

In this section, you will find the traits to look for in the people that can help you leapfrog over the mistakes people made the first time around. Hard work is key to your success, but make sure you ask people who have already done what you want to do, how to do it. Sometimes these people may be hard to find, in this chapter you will find out where to go and how to get the most out of a relationship. You will also learn how to maintain a good relationship with your mentor. Learning from experts is key early on.

Chapter 3: Be Courageous

I was determined to make money and find a business that would work. I felt like I tried it all, from network marketing, commission sales, even a clothing company in my early twenties that people thought I was *crazy*! The amount of people that said, "Nice head, Hogben," would make your head spin. In this chapter you will see how failing is a good thing, and that just because one thing does not work out it does not mean that the next opportunity will be a failure too. Get courageous and fail fast, as the faster you fail the sooner success will be around the corner for you.

Chapter 4: Buy Real Estate Now

In this chapter you will learn about what type of real estate to purchase and what are the best options for you to accelerate your Mission. There are many different ways to make money in real estate, you can buy and hold, fix and flip, or joint venture with people, the trick is starting now. This chapter was crucial to me building my wealth and getting to my Mission35 destination. Had I not purchased real estate I would not be where I am today. After reading this chapter you will have the confidence to leap into your next real estate deal with both feet. The perfect time to buy real estate is now!

Chapter 5: Work Hard and Condense Your Career

In this chapter you will learn how to maximize 168 hours in the week.
I wish I could say there was a real sweet and easy secret sauce for your
Mission, but unfortunately, nothing compares to hard work. There were
multiple times in my early career where I wanted to quit and try something
else. Instead, I dug my nose in and worked harder than others were willing
to. Hard work does pay off! You will learn how to manage your time, and
ensure you have your priorities straight and in line with where you want
to go.

Chapter 6: Invest Your Money, Don't Save Your Money

There is a misconception that you should save, save, save! Put your money
away and you can get a nice 2-3% return on your money! *Bullshit.* Take
the time to learn something that you are passionate about, put your money
into it, and then make it grow. Don't let someone else make it grow for
you! In this chapter, I'll show you where you should be investing your
money, and how much of it in each asset category.

Chapter 7: Start a Business and Work for Yourself

I learned early on in my banking career that I would never make the money
I deserved working for someone else. In this chapter you will quickly see
that no matter what your occupation you need to have a part time small
business. I will show you the benefits of your income growing in your own
business, and a couple of nice tax saving as well.

Chapter 8: Reward Yourself Along the Way

It will be hard to focus on a goal that is five, ten, or even fifteen years
in the future, so make sure you set some milestones along the way and
celebrate the hell out of them. You *should* be rewarded for your hard work
and efforts. In this chapter you will get your creative juices flowing on
what rewards you are looking for, and how to ensure you celebrate them
when you reach them. I bought my first sports car at twenty-nine, after I
had broke the $200,000 mark in my income earnings. This was something
I so desperately wanted, and it gave me something to enjoy while I was on
my Freedom Journey.

Chapter 9: Focus Your Efforts

This journey you are on is about choices. The better ones you make, the better off you will be. In this chapter you will learn what to focus your energy on. I will show you how to truly master your craft in order to get more money and excitement. When you focus on one thing, you will be able to constantly reinvent your occupation, and you won't end up being the person who has one year of experience ten times!

Chapter 10: Giving Back Keeps You Grounded

In this chapter you will learn about what charity gives to you, giving can be selfish, who knew? You want to ensure that you do not become a money-loving monster! It can happen. Your goals will be big, but you must always remember the less fortunate out there and when you are not reaching your goals, it will be good to keep yourself grounded to see that others have *way* less than you do. Contribution to others is a basic human need that will help you on your Mission.

Chapter 11: Attitude: Pick a Good One!

In this last chapter you will identify how to keep a positive attitude. There will be so many people who will shoot you down along the way—more than those who will pick you up. How you look at your life and your goals will dictate your success.

Chapter 1:
Goals

Your goals are your future.

"Keep your goals out of reach, but not out of sight."

Most people spend fifty weeks of the year planning two—and this is completely backwards!

Each year, I always spent my vacations lounging by a pool, ocean, or lake, usually someplace hot, planning out how my life was going to look. My beautiful wife would be catching up with the latest trash mags while I would be setting my goals for the next ninety days, one year, and five years. I would write out lists and make plans like a maniac, always planning out how I wanted my life to look. This is a strategy I never stopped; even as I type this out, I am sitting in a beautiful condo on Flamingo Beach in Costa Rica.

I truly believe your best thoughts and ideas flow from you when you take your head out of the sand. It is almost impossible to plan for your life while you are working in it. By the time you put in your eight to twelve hours of work in a day and spend time with your loved ones, your kids, and your spouse, you *must* be exhausted. How can you plan your life when you have spent your best hours busy at work? I have set my schedule so that we are on a one-week vacation every three months. Of course, it wasn't always this way; as I was not able to take as many vacations when I was building my business. When I was young, I would always take a Saturday morning (when I wasn't too hung over) and write out lists of what I wanted to do, and what I wanted my future to look like. At the very least, over the Christmas holidays, before getting into the rum and egg nog, I would spend at least two days writing out what I wanted my goals to look like and what I wanted to accomplish in the coming year.

This type of direction lets me give my all to everything. I am more focused and patient, and I am able to truly focus my energy on what I want to do. It is so easy to get distracted if you have not taken the time to plan out where you are going. If you do not set any goals, then how will you know when you arrive where you are going? From the age of seventeen, my goal was Mission 35. What "Mission 35" meant to me was being in a place where I could choose to do what I want, when I want—and where I could be in a position of not *having* to do anything. I never imagined I would stop working at age thirty-five; I love to work, I love to grow, and I love to be challenged. I do love vacations, but I could not sit on a beach for the rest of my life. I wanted to have financial security.

I have read hundreds of books and gone to countless seminars on goal-setting—how to do it, how not to, and so on. The idea is, just make sure you do it! Take the time and write your goals down. If you just think about them, they are still a thought in the universe. As soon as you write them down they become real, and they become intentional. When I was young, I used to write my goals down over the Christmas holidays and not look at them until the end of the following year. I would say to myself, "Oh yeah, that was important to me. Idiot!"

Your goals are your roadmap, and you should keep them some place where you can continually look at them and remind yourself why you are doing all the shitty things that you are doing some days. Take a picture and make it your screensaver on your phone to remind yourself of what is important. Today, my screensaver is my baby girl Lyla staring back at me with her tongue sticking out. She is the reason that I keep pushing myself to do more, as I want her to be proud of her dad. By having her on my smart phone I am constantly reminded of why I am pushing forward. Make sure you read your goals *every* day; if you don't, you will forget what is important to you.

There was a study of a hundred Harvard business grads. Only 10% of them actually wrote out goals—one-year, five-year, and ten-year goals. When the hundred grads were interviewed twenty-five years later, the 10% who wrote out their goals had a net worth that was greater than the other 90% combined! I cannot stress how important this exercise is. It truly does make a difference. Without goals, it is like getting in the car and starting to drive with absolutely no destination or plan. Where are you going to stop for gas? Is there food where you are going? The more detailed the plan, the easier it will be to get there. You are only fooling yourself if you get in the car, turn the ignition, but don't set the GPS for your destination. When you arrive at where you are going, you will just tell yourself, "This is good." If you're striving for anything, you will surely achieve it. It's better to know what you are going for—not only that, but the clearer picture you paint for yourself, the more likely you are to arrive there.

Once you write out your goals, if you really want to step it up, tell someone about them. When you tell someone about them—and not just some stranger on the street, but someone you care about, love, and trust—you have now made yourself accountable. This person can also help be your navigator, and if you are heading off-course, they can point you back in the right direction. If no one is aware of the final destination, then how can they point out that you made a wrong turn somewhere? Being accountable opens up the conversation, especially with someone you care about, to keep you motivated and on track.

What Happened

A dream board was one of the coolest things I had done when I was young. It was like a visual goal-setting sheet. I was told to find a bunch of magazines and cut out any pictures of things that I thought I wanted in my life, or how I wanted my future to look, and put them together in a collage on a big sheet of paper. I did not have Pinterest back in those days. It seemed like a cheesy, meaningless project when it was explained to me, but the effect is quite powerful. Whatever you focus on will come into your reality. When you write down the goal, make sure to have pictures to associate with it, as well. Manifested on the dream board, the goal will be constantly in the forefront of your mind. By knowing what your looking for via the dream board your RAS (Reticular Activating System), which is part of the brain, is subconsciously on the hunt to help you achieve your goals. The RAS is what causes you to look for something when you don't normally look for it. For example, if you wanted to buy a black Range Rover, you might all of a sudden start noticing them everywhere; they may have always been around in the past, but now you are aware of them. By having your goals clearly outlined in front of you, your brain will look for ways to help you get them.

When I was twenty-four, I started working in a "networking marketing company." This was a company where they sold products such as dish soap, toothpaste, toilet paper, and other household goods. Can you picture my friends at the time? They were like, "Um, Brian, I live at home with my parents. Why the hell do I want to buy overpriced toilet paper from you?" Talk about a good question! My goal at the time was to retire and make $10,000 a month selling toilet paper. Okay—maybe it wasn't the best goal in the world, but at least it was a start, and it gave me something to shoot for. The beautiful thing about having a goal is that sometimes things happen to you while you're trying to achieve a goal, and these incidental things are actually more important than the goal itself. After months of not selling anything—except for the amazing toilet paper I purchased for myself at a terribly inflated price—I realized that what I was learning was how to sell. My goal to make money in this business was teaching me one of the most valuable lessons I could have learned in life: *facing rejection!* Man, not only did no one buy anything, but the amount that people made fun of me for selling dish soap made it hard to get a good date.

However, the dream board was first introduced to me through this network marketing company. I thought, *What a stupid idea*, but I went along with it anyway. I wrote a million dollar cheque on it, put a picture of my friends on it, and there was a picture of a guy holding a surfboard, and the caption read "board meeting." There was another picture of a man standing in the middle of a desert in front of three distinctly different roads, and the caption read, "The hardest thing to do if you can do anything, is to do anything." There was a picture of an Audi, as well as a BMW. There were pictures of massive pieces of real estate, soaring skyscrapers, and beautiful buildings. These all represented to me my dream of owning lots of real estate. All of these things were always in the forefront of my mind when I was having "tea parties," inviting people twice my age over and trying to sell prestigious household goods while they looked at me thinking, *I feel so bad for this kid*—but not bad enough to buy anything! Every time I got rejection—which was *a lot*—I always looked at my dream board and thought, *This is just a minor hiccup in my road to greatness.* It allowed me to always see the forest for the trees. I hung the dream board in my office and made sure that I looked at it constantly. Luckily for me, I didn't quit my day job at the bank to sell toilet paper, but instead I took what I was learning in the form of setting goals and started applying it to other aspects of my life. Thank god!

What To Do

I believe there are four main categories that you should be focusing on for your goals: financial, family, health, and hobbies (fun). They are all equally important, and I am going to give you an action plan for each one. Hitting all your financial goals means nothing if you are sick and dying at thirty-five years old, *or* if you have no family or friends to share them with. If you don't have any hobbies or fun, then what is the point, anyways? The more fun you have in your journey, the more reason you will have to pursue those adventures.

Financial

This is the meat and potatoes of what you are looking for. When you are looking at getting to a goal of redefining your retirement and hitting financial security, I want you to have a certain number in mind. This is the main number I want you to focus on and it is the ultimate destination of where you want your net wroth to be when you hit your Mission

That number is your FIA number, which is your overall Mission. Your FIA is what you want your net worth to be by the time you reach your

Mission date. (your net worth, simply put, is everything you own minus everything you owe). This is what I affectionately call your "Fuck It All" number—or, for you PG-13ers out there, "Forget It All." When you have this number as your net worth, you can say "forget you" to the job you hate or the boss you loathe. You can say "forget you" to commuting to work, and to not having enough time to see your spouse on your anniversary dinner. You can say "forget you" to being on call over holidays, and missing your son's hockey tournament or your daughter's dance recital. The FIA number is your financial security number. This number will allow you to have all of your basic needs met, such as your housing, car, utilities, and basic entertainment. This is not your financial "freedom" number, where you can do anything anytime. By having financial security you are able to open up your mind to possibilities for all that you want in your life. . If you are not thinking about money, which can take up a lot of your thoughts throughout a month, a week and even a day, what could you put your mind energy too? Financial security or your FIA will not only help you flex your creative muscles but also build your courage.

Now, in order to calculate your FIA number, see Figure 1A below. I have included a sample of my FIA number calculation as well, titled "Brian's." Here are some things to think about before you jump in.

When do I want to achieve financial security or your FIA? For me it was on my 35th birthday, for you it could be 45, 55, or 25. Pick a year now in which you would like to have it.

What is the value of a house that you could live in today? Not the value of your dream home that you have a picture saved on your home screen. This is a home that if you never had to work another day in your life you would be happy living in. You can always strive for more, but this is coming from a place of absolute financial security for yourself.

What are your basic monthly living expenses? These are your needs, not your wants. Such as your car expenses, insurance, food, house expenses and utilities.

What are your current monthly fun expenses? Now this is not your dream vacation plans, it is what you actually spend now in a year on fun. If you go on 1 amazing all inclusive vacation in the year, at a cost of $6000 than your monthly fun expenses would be approx. $500 per month. If you rent a cottage in the summer for a week for a total cost of $3000 and go on a vacation for $6000 in the winter than your monthly cost would be $6000+$3000 = $9000/12 = $750 per month. Financial security, or your FIA number is your "basic" entertainment, not living the baller lifestyle that you will most surely have after you hit your FIA number.

Lastly you will calculate the number of months that you have from you Mission date until the age of 65. For example, if you have a Mission date of 45, you would have 20 years until you hit the age of 65, which would equate to 20x12 = 240 months. This calculation gives you the number of months that you would need the income for until you hit the age of 65.

Figure 1A – Brian's

Primary Residence Value	***$400,000***
Monthly Living Expenses	$2,000
Plus	
Monthly Fun Expenses	$2,000
Total Expenses	$4,000
Total Monthly Expenses (# of months until the age of 65 from your desired Mission Age) **65 – 35 = 30years x 12 = 360** **This number is 360 months of my monthly living and fun expenses.**	***$1,440,000***
FIA Number	**$1,840,000**

Now it is your turn to give it a try! Remember: this is for the ability to say "forget you" to all of the commitments you hate. If you set your goals too unrealistically, you will become unmotivated and deflated, and you'll think that it will never happen. This is your financial security number not your financial freedom number. I used to confuse the 2 for a long time, and it can be extremely discouraging if you are thinking about absolute financial freedom as that is exponentially higher than your financial security number. The freedom number includes chartered jets, backstage passes and unlimited palm tree holidays. The security number is your basic needs met.

I do believe that striving for more is great; however, in order to achieve your Mission, you have to be realistic. A house that you *can* live in means having enough bedrooms and bathrooms for your family in a neighbourhood where, if you have kids, they can go to school without getting shot on the way. Seriously though, this should be a nice neighbourhood where you can see yourself raising a family, if that is what is important to you. If you are in a dead-end job, or your boss is an absolute A-hole, you may actually not mind moving and downsizing from your mansion to a place that has no mortgage on it and allows you to walk your kids to and from school, because leaving a job you hate, will be more important to you than keeping up with the Joneses!

Now, record the value of the house you "can" live in under the "Primary Residence" in the diagram that says "Figure 1A – Yours." Once you have your principal residence number picked out, we are going to look at your monthly expenses, as well. See Figure 2A for a sample of my budget for this category.

Figure 2A – Brian

Property Taxes	$300
Utilities	$500
Cell Phone	$100
Internet	$100
Car Insurance	$150
Gas	$100
Groceries	$450
Miscellaneous	$300

$2,000 per month

Now, the assumption here is that you have no mortgage. You are moving into a property that is mortgage-free. If you still have a mortgage than you must account for the mortgage payment costs. This is also under the assumption that you have no debt! Therefore, all the money you have is actually going towards living expenses or fun. Depending on your situation right now, you may be renting and have no idea what utilities are, so you can ask your parents/friends and see what it is, if that relates to you. The idea in this category is to give you an idea of how much it will cost you to live every month. Again, be realistic. Do not include feeding your five purebred horses in this category, even if you are a horse lover, as there will be some sacrifices that you have to make in order to choose a lifestyle that suits your Mission. Fill in the numbers as best you can for where you see your situation based on the house you *can* live in.

Figure 2A – Yours

Property Taxes	$ _____
Utilities	$ _____
Cell Phone	$ _____
Internet	$ _____
Car Insurance	$ _____
Gas	$ _____
Groceries	$ _____
Miscellaneous	$ _____
Total	$ _____ per month

Now, the good stuff: you need to figure out your monthly fun expense! Figure 3A is my personal example of what works for me. In my example, you can see that I have allocated $500 per month or $6,000 per year for snowboarding. As I live in Canada, this will probably be more of a winter fun activity for me, so I can allocate those funds as $1,000 per month for six months, or $2,000 in three months if I desire. This would be the same if you love golf. Personally, I am terrible at it, and no amount of practice (even in my retirement) will help me get better at it, so I gave up. The same is true for my travel expenses; I would most likely not spend $1000 per month on a vacation, but I may be tempted to go scuba diving in Belize once every three months, and that would equate to $3,000 for that trip. Again, being realistic in this category is paramount to your success. If you want to go heli-skiing in the Swiss Alps once a month, you are going to have an astronomical fun expense. When you calculate it out, it will be such a ridiculous number that you will say "forget you" become discouraged and make up excuses as to why you can not make it to your Mission.

Figure 3A

Activity	Scuba Diving	$500 per month
Activity	Snow boarding	$500 per month
Activity	Travel	$1000 per month
Total		$2000 per month

Now, if you are having trouble with this exercise, you need to have more fun! A good standard is to look at the holidays that you have taken over the past year and increase it by 25%, in both time and budget. If you have not travelled much, or taken much time off during your working years, you will surprisingly find it tough to all of sudden change into a completely different person who spends all their time jet-setting across the world. If you goal is to travel the world at thirty-five and spend six months working and six months travelling, then where do you want to be travelling, and how much will that cost? Perhaps that means living in a condo that you rent out six months of the year through Airbnb and travelling the other six months. I'm just giving you some ideas to get those creative juices flowing!

Take some time now and fill out "Figure 3A – Yours" below. Have some fun with it, and remember, it can change as you change, as well. The idea here is to get to your FIA number.

Figure 3A – Yours

Activity _____ $ _____

Activity _____ $ _____

Activity _____ $ _____

Activity _____ $ _____

Activity _____ $ _____

Total $ _____ per month

Now you are ready to find out your FIA number! Fill in all the total numbers in the "Figure 1A – Yours" if you have not already jumped ahead. Take the monthly living and fun expenses, add them up, and multiply them by the number of months from your mission date to the age 65. The Mission date is how old you are on your birthday when you hit your FIA number. This is the date you picked for your Financial Security. This should be the date you throw a huge party, I sure did. In my case my Mission age was 35, so it was 65 – 35 which is 30 years x 12 = 360 months. I needed to have 360 months of my basic needs covered in order to have my financial security.) Add to this the primary residence value, and you have your number. If you need help, email us at info@mi35.com

Figure 1A – Yours

Primary Residence Value $_____

Monthly Living Expenses $_____

Plus

Monthly Fun Expenses $_____

Total Expenses $_____

Total Monthly Expenses
X Number of months from now
until your Mission Date $_____

FIA Number
(Add the Number from the total monthly
expenses to the Primary residence value.) $_____

This gives me a value of $1,840,000. This is my Fuck It All number, my financial security number, meaning that if I choose to give up on responsibilities and sell all of my investments (real estate and what not), I can put all of my funds into a very conservative investment and make 3-4% on my money and have enough to survive on until I am well into my 70s. This doesn't even take into consideration any Canada Pension Plan or Old Age Security pension income that currently I am *supposed* to get from the government; it remains to be seen if any of these funds will be available at the time we get to the age in which we can receive them. In addition to any of you naysayers out there, this does not even take into consideration the monthly interest you would get on your investments.

Once you have your FIA number, stop for a moment, and maybe have a glass of wine to help you digest it! It will, in most cases, be absolutely huge! That is okay, as the idea here is to bring it into your awareness so that you know what you need to do. I would also bet for some of you it is not as big as you thought it might be! You see financial security is very often mis-represented with financial freedom. When you have financial security you can operate from a mindset of abundance instead of scarcity, as you are not worried about paying the bills you know they will be paid no matter what. So with money taken care of, if you want to shoot for absolute financial freedom, then go for it! Get the jet and all the bling that comes with it. I guarantee you, as I am living proof, that it is easier to take more risks once you have this in your back pocket to fall back on.

Now, take that FIA number and divide it into the number of years you have until you reach your Mission date. Keep that wine handy, as it might not get and rosier here! This may seem like a daunting number at first, especially the later on you are on your Mission. If you are too overwhelmed try the exercise again but make your Mission date 2-3 years later, make sure you get a number that seems realistic and possible to you. Something to keep in mind is that your assets will grow exponentially as you accumulate them. For example, you may only be able to accumulate a fraction of your goal in the first several years. If you follow the steps outlined, you will see miraculous momentum in the accumulation of your assets. For example, when you get to the million mark in assets, if they grow by 6% in a year, that is $60,000 before you add any of your own savings. Through the use of the budget, you will be able to achieve this number. If this were Mission 65 you would not feel any pressure at all, but that is likely the Mission you may be on now. By utilizing the teaching in this chapter and the ones to come, you will find that it will all come together and you will be able to have it all by your target Mission date.

Your FIA is a very different goal-setting exercise than what you may be used to; it actually went against many of the teachings I had, but it is very strategic. Most people will tell you "Shoot for the stars," or my favourite, "Fake it till you make it!" But this is bullshit! If you are trying to fake it all the way, then you will be spending money on things that are not truly important. People will respect you more when you are actually making sacrifices in order to achieve your mission. I never once lost a mortgage deal in my career because I drove a Ford Escape. I remember doing my biggest deal for a stockbroker who had a T4 income of $4 million per year! When I pulled up to his house and he saw my car, he smiled at me and said, "You seem like an honest, hard-working guy." Damn right—I wasn't some wannabe douchebag who was pretending to be something he wasn't.

Once you find out how to live within your means, and have the funds and money to support that lifestyle you have financial security taken care of in your life, you can be a no-holds-barred risk-taker and go after the stars! That is how I always looked at things, as now, if you don't want to work with me, it's "No problem!" I tell people all the time that "I know I will take care of you, but if you don't see the value in what I am selling, then you don't have to buy it!" It is such a freeing mental space to live in. I can take exponentially *more* risks than anyone else I know now, as I have the confidence that I can live comfortably if I fall flat on my face. The FIA is your security, and everything else is the gravy. That is another reason why I only account for income until the age of sixty-five, as when you are free, you *will* make more money than you ever have before. When you operate in absolute confidence, people will be drawn to you, because you are not financially tied to the outcome. If it works *great*, if not, *great*. I am doing what I do because I love it, and I know my family is already taken care of.

Next, on to budgeting: In order to meet your goals and your FIA number, you need the tools on how to manage your money. You need to learn it now, for when you make more money, it doesn't get easier to manage—it simply can compound your problems exponentially! My dad used to always say, "If you're broke making $40,000 per year, you will be broke making $400,000 per year." In short, more money will magnify your money-management problems.

Budgeting is something that people have agonized over for years. You start out great with amazing intentions, and then before you know it, some expenses come up, you treat yourself with a new purse, and it all goes out the window. I am going to teach you a simple budget to follow for all of your income to flow through, regardless of whether you have a salary, hourly, commission-based, or self-employed income. All of your income—even your birthday money—has to flow through this budget, and it will take out all of the inconsistencies you have with your emotional spending habits.

The budget is broken down into six categories: necessities, long-term savings for spending, fun, investing, gifts, and debt repayment. (If you are self-employed or commissioned-based, there is an additional category for income taxes.) Each of the categories is assigned a percentage of your income. This is for *all* the income that you get, including birthday money, graduation gifts, bonuses, etc.

For step-by-step video instructions on budgeting, check out our Mission 35 Education plan at www.mission35.com

1. *Necessities*
The ideal amount is 40% of your net income. This is for the expenses you have right now that you need to pay for in order to meet your basic needs. Included here are groceries, gas, car insurance, mortgage payment, utilities, cell phone, etc. A necessity is not getting your hair professionally done once a week (although my wife would beg to differ). This category should account for no more than 40% of your net income. Your net income is the income you get after taxes and any payroll deductions.

2. *Long-term savings for spending*
The ideal amount is 15% of your net income. This is typically where people go way off target with there budget. Either they blow through their savings dollars *or* go into major debt. This category includes the trip or family vacation you are planning for this year. This could also be for the new car you are looking to get. This category accounts for 15% of your net income. By continually saving in this category, you will not go into debt for the expenses that "seem" to creep up. The reality is that they were always there—you just never accounted for them. You don't go on the trip till you have the funds. You don't buy the car till you have the funds. I saved for my sports car for years!

3. *Fun*
The ideal amount is 10% of your net income. The fun category is money that you get to spend guilt-free every month! In fact, you have to spend it guilt-free every month, because if you don't, you will have an unbalanced financial situation. This category accounts for 10% of your net income. Don't neglect yourself in this category; you need to have fun. This is the

most important category. It will challenge you to spend money on the things that are really important, *and* to find things that you can do for fun that do not cost a lot of money. Saving for something really big in your "long-term savings for spending" budget will actually bring you more joy when you do, and it will be much more gratifying than when you put it on a credit card.

I remember putting my first all-inclusive trip to Punta Cana on a credit card when I had approximately $25,000 of student debt already, and halfway through the trip I was feeling shitty over the concern of how I was going to pay it off again; then I was robbing myself of things I wanted to do on the trip because I knew I would have to go deeper into debt. A debt-free vacation is the *best* type of vacation no matter where it is! Plan and budget for your trips, and they will be the best trips you ever have, and you will be the best *you* on the trip as well, with no black shadow of guilt hanging over your shoulder.

4. *Investing*

The ideal amount is 15% of net income. This is important to learn fast and get used to. The age-old advice of "Pay off all your debt first" then start building your investments is *bullshit!* I have learned that on your Freedom Journey you will always have some sort of debt, so learn to manage it emotionally and strategically. I know that when you get a bonus or a big paycheque and you make a monster payment on a credit card if feels soooooooo good. It releases some endorphins in your body, and you are a debt-paying machine! You are a rock star and you have all your money under control . . . for a few days, weeks, or months. Then, like a big sting, it hits you. You think, *I deserve to go on a trip, buy that dress, get those shoes*, or whatever your vice may be. Then you are out charging up the credit card again, because *damn it*, you work hard and you deserve it! This is what I call your emotional financial roller coaster. You pay off debt, pay off debt, and pay off debt, and then you charge the credit cards right back up again! This is the reason you need to have a percentage of your money working for you *all the time*; the sooner you start to grow your assets by investing money, the sooner you can start making money while you are sleeping, which is the ultimate goal. I had a mentor tell me once, "You can get rich working at your job. However, it will be your investments that make you wealthy." This was some of the best advice I ever got. Start investing now, whether you are $1,000 in debt or $100,000 in debt.

5. *Gifts*

The ideal amount is 5% of your net income. This is one category that always ate into my finances, and it was super annoying to me, as I never budgeted for it when I was young. Gifts are the things you get for your boyfriend, wife, kids, friends for their birthdays, anniversaries, Christmas, graduations, you name it. By having a budget for it, you have an amount that you are allowed to spend, and so you are not overspending on gifts. I remember forgetting my first long-term girlfriend's birthday, and at the last minute I bought her a $400 gift card for a spa online, while she was in the other room. I didn't have $400 to spend, but that was how much room I had on my credit card, so that is what I spent. She didn't even like the spa I got it from! Guilt can cause you *a lot* of money—not to mention grief, especially if she breaks up with you shortly after.

I used to think the amount I spent on a gift was a direct correlation of how much I cared about someone; but this is not the case! Some of the best gifts I have ever received were personal notes, letters, or things that had sentimental value. My wife got me a calendar for Christmas that was full of pictures of our six-month-old daughter—a different picture for each month. It probably cost $25 to put together, as well as her time (which is the most precious), and it was the *best* thing I got for Christmas. Budget for your gifts, or your budget will slowly bleed out money.

6. *Debt Repayment*

The ideal amount is 15% of your net income. All of your money should not be going into this category. Learn to live with it. I know it hurts, and you want to release the happy juice in your body by making a big payment, but don't do it! As with the investments, be strategic and disciplined with how much you are putting towards this. Simply put your allotted percentage each month towards your personal debts—no more and no less. Go to your bank and consolidate to a low-interest line of credit, loan, or credit card, and make your payments. *Always* make your minimum payments at the very least, as a good credit rating is your number-one tool in your belt in order to build your wealth. The goal is to eliminate *all* of your bad debt. Simply put, "bad debt" is debt that is not tax deductible against your income. This is your credit card for the trips you took or the shopping spree, your student loans, even the mortgage on your primary residence. The mortgage you have on your house should be the last debt you tackle. Even though you should be purchasing a house, the one you live in is not tax deductible. Once you pay it off and *reborrow* the money off of your house for an investment property or business venture, it will then become tax deductible.

If you are seriously struggling in this category, email us at info@ mission35.com and we will put you in touch with some great debt advisors in order to get you on track. Bankruptcy and Consumer Proposals are things that are very common in this day and age, and it may be the necessary step in order to move you forward. Not addressing your situation will not make it any better. The sooner you take a step, the sooner you can get out of the crappy situation you may be in. I have seen many people file for a bankruptcy and within seven years be *well* on their way to their FIA number.

Now, if your percentages for each budgeting category are spot on, then give yourself a huge pat on the back, because you are way above the average Joe! If not, grab that wine again (which you cracked open during the FIA number calculation) as you have some work to do. This whole chapter is the toughest one to grasp, but it does get easier. What you are doing is zeroing in on your financial GPS, locating exactly where you are and raising this knowledge into your reality. This is the step most people don't get to in their entire lives! Find out where you are right now by taking the last two months of your online banking and filling out the starting point in your budget. Email us at info@mi35.com for an Excel copy.

By knowing where you are, you can start to take steps in order to get you to the desired percentages. Do not—I repeat, *do not*—try to fit your existing expenses into this budget right away, as it will not work. You have spent your whole life living one way with your finances, and it will not change overnight. Try to improve your percentage by 5% at a time over a three-month period. If you are like me, you are probably starting with

"fun" at 40% and "necessities" at 60% and "debt repayment" at 40%. If ·
you are paying attention, you will realize that this adds up to *more* than
100%! This is okay; start from wherever you are and make strides towards
improvement. It will come with time. Be patient and stick with it.

*If you are wondering where to put all those cash withdrawals you see on your
online banking, don't kid yourself—that was "fun" money. Start accounting for
where all your cash goes.*

Family:

Make sure to write down who is important in your life—meaning, your
family and friends. Make sure you have a list of no more than ten individuals, but at least five. The younger you are the harder this list will be to
make, but the key here is to ensure you are surrounding yourself with loved
ones who will support you, and who you want to spend time with. They
say your average income will be that of your five closest friends. Be sure to
surround yourself with those like-minded individuals, as they will cheer
you on, *and* more importantly, they will keep you accountable!

Health:

This is a tough one, as I didn't start thinking of my health until I hit thirty.
Before that, I thought I was invincible and that I was going to live forever!
The idea in this category when you're young is to stay active; by staying
active, you will have more energy, and the more energy you have, the better
focused you will be on your goals. They say you have to exercise your body
before you exercise your mind, and I could not agree more! Find something that works for you, and stick to it. I love to run on the weekends
and once during the week with one of my best friends. We will meet up at
lunch time, which is fun to break up the day, and go for a 5km jog. This is
actually fulfilling 2 of my categories as he has been a friend of mine since
I was in kindergarten. This is something that keeps me active and it *gives*
me energy.

Hobbies:

Lastly, this is the "fun" category! What do you like to do for fun, and how do you want to be spending your time when you do retire? Make sure you account at least five hours a week to this category. It can be hard to find hobbies if you forget about them. I had this specific issue, and when I turned thirty, I had to actually rediscover what I liked to do. I had forgotten about these activities! I know now that I love running, scuba diving, reading, and travelling, and I am quite the foodie, as well.

Remember that your goals for family and health is not static; it will be ever-changing. You *need* to have the people in your life who will cheer you on. You know who the naysayers are in your life, and one of the toughest things you will have to do is *cut them out*; the more time you spend with them, the more they will make you feel *bad* about some of the sacrifices you will have to make. They will say things like, "You only live once," and "You work too much"—which, to me, is complete bullshit. You're right—I *do* only live once, and I want to make this the best life possible while I am young and have boundless energy. I want to make all the right choices to ensure that I will take care of my future today, and so that I can have all the *fun* I want while you are still working! People will shoot you down only because it makes them feel better about their own choices for being lazy or not committing to a mission. People say things for themselves; rarely do they say things for you. You'll find that the ones who do will be your biggest advocates, and they will be the ones racing with you on your path to freedom.

Chapter 2:
Mentors

Mentors allow you to leapfrog your way to success.

*"A mentor is someone who allows you
to see the hope inside yourself."*
—*Oprah Winfrey*

Mentors are the ones in your life who have already done what you want to do, or they are the ones who have the life that you want to have. They are everywhere—both good and bad. Mentors allow you to learn the lesson—if you are paying attention, of course—without actually having to make the colossal mistake that they probably did. They allow you to leapfrog over the massive fuck-up that they made and go right on into the learning and the lesson of what has happened. You will know great mentors when you see them, as they will be interested in you, and they will be happy to share their knowledge with you. When you come across a mentor that you truly want to learn from, be respectful and prepare to spend time with them. They will be happy to help you, so long as you respect their time and who they are. Be like a sponge and get as much info as you can from them. Be on the lookout for these people, and be sure to keep them as close to you in your life as possible. You want them to become your friends as life goes by. As the saying goes, "Your income will be the average of your three closest friends." Some of you may be saying, "Helllll no," but the reality is that you are who you associate with. People who make $30,000 a year have $30,000-a-year problems. People who make $300,000 a year have $300,000-a-year problems—and you get the idea. Someone who is making $3 million dollars a year is not likely to be complaining about gas prices. (Unless, of course, they own an airline, and the cost of doing business just went up).

You can have different mentors for different lessons. Someone who is an excellent sales person may not be the best mentor on health and fitness. Be sure to know what you are choosing your mentor for, and do not confuse the fact that you have to be like them in every facet of their life. If you want to learn money management skills from Warren Buffet, that is one thing, but perhaps he may not be the best at parenthood. (I personally don't know, but would think that if Warren Buffet was you *dad* you would have some pretty damn good perks that might make up for any shortcomings!)

Some of the best mentors can also be found in books. I remember reading books by Robert Kiyosaki, Napoleon Hill, and Tony Robbins, to name a few. They all changed my life for different reasons at different times. They enabled me to start looking at life differently, when not too many other people in my sphere of influence were. Books and audios can sometimes be even better than the real deal, as you can learn at you own pace and listen to them over and over again. I am a huge believer in reading; I truly believe the statement that "Leaders are readers." These books and authors acted as my mentors, and they still do.

I believe you should listen to an inspirational audio or read an uplifting book for at least fifteen minutes per day. There is so much negativity in the world that I equate it to taking a shower. You shower every day to get the dirt off of you (at least I hope you do—if not, you have some bigger fish to fry), so why would you not take a "mind shower" and wash all the negative shit off of you that people say to you every day? "You can't do this," they say, or "You can't do that," or "You're a dreamer," or "Put that gun down . . ." (okay, I was just seeing if you were still paying attention). Even the news today is *very* unlikely to have any good news stories on it! However, listening and reading on a daily basis will help you to believe that what you want to do is possible. The real-life mentors will not be stuck to you by your side every day, and if you are lucky to speak with them once a week, I think you are doing great. So ensure you have a system in place to read or listen *every day*!

Now I will introduce my four main mentors—Frank, Barry, John, and Peter Hogben—and explain the valuable lessons that they taught me.

What Happened

I had just become a Personal Banking Officer at a major Canadian bank when I met Frank. He came in to replace an old manager right at the time I received a promotion. I thought I was hot shit and knew it all, but when I met Frank, I quickly realized I had a lot to learn. He was the first person I met (outside of my family) who I had worked for who really had *my* best interests at heart. He was a salesman through and through. He would get business and give it to me to process—and I would get the credit for it! Wow, what a generous guy. He was also able to identify that after two years in the personal banking role, I wasn't happy and wanted more. He put me in touch with my next mentor, Barry, to do a 100% commission-based role. He did this selflessly, and it was something that I wasn't used to nor had seen before, especially in the corporate banking world. In hindsight, Frank was probably the busiest guy I knew at the time, and you would never know it. Truly, his door was *always* open; he would always make time for me, he would put on a smile, and he would always make me feel like I was the most important thing to him at that moment in time. What a gift he had.

Frank was a legend at the bank; one of his claims to fame was how he singlehandedly managed to have the safety deposit box rules rewritten across the country. He had opened up a safety deposit box for a client who had not paid, and when he opened it, all of its contents happened to spill out onto the desk. What he didn't realize was that there were some very expensive hockey card collectables that were in the safe, and when they fell onto the desk, they were slightly damaged. For you hard-core collectors out there, this is a problem, as you want the cards in pristine condition. The clients naturally complained and even went to the newspapers, and Frank made the front page as the mean old bank manager who was destroying some kid's future. Instead of taking it as a huge hit to his career, and trying to hide from the event. He boastfully told people that because of him, the bank had to re write their policy for safekeeping in the bank vault. He was able to spin this fiasco into something positive that he contributed to. Re writing bank policy is a pretty tall order if you ask me. Again—what a guy.

What I Made It Mean

I learned that this was someone that I needed to stay in touch with *forever*! His open-door policy, total open communication, and support for me was unbelievable. I realized, for the first time, that there actually were people in the workforce who wanted to see you succeed; I also realized that there were people who weren't just out for themselves and making themselves look good. Frank went on to be a director for the bank in the head office, where he continues to break records. His devotion to people and truly doing what is best for hem taught me that the secret in business is not "give to get"; rather, it is to "give, give, give, and then give some more"—*period*! Frank never asked anything from me except to do my best. He understood that you can't keep good people down for your own selfish reasons (as many managers will do in the workforce today). When you have a good person, a good worker, or whatever they may be, teach them all you can, and they will perform well; you never know how the karma from this will come back to you later in life. Knowing that you did what was right for someone will stay with you longer than the temporary results of holding someone back for your own advancement.

What To Do

No matter what business you are in, be like Frank and always give to your employees, customers, and co-workers. You will never be able to keep good people down, so why not try and make them all excel? Authentically having their best interests at heart is the best policy. When this happens, people can feel it, and the reciprocity you will see in return will be limitless. When you base your reputation on giving, it will cascade throughout your industry over time, and you will be the one that people will trust when it comes to a hard decision or opportunity.

We actually have a ten-year policy in our mortgage company today. I want everyone that works with me to be able to retire in ten years. I will work with our employees on there finances in order to help them grow different income streams to help them generate a passive income while they are working with Mission35. This links directly back to Frank always wanting to see people excel, and genuinely having their lively hood at heart. By Frank giving so much unselfishly to me, I would always be there for him if he needed anything. This is a type of loyalty that was truly earned through his efforts, and I want to earn the same with my co workers. If they are able to reach there Mission I will know I did my part like Frank and contributed time, knowledge and value to the relationship.

Frank was an amazing mentor to me, and he's an amazing friend still to this day. He did some of the simplest things that stayed with me for so long: thanking people for their business, connecting with people, always making time for people, and always having an open door. These were things that came naturally to Frank.

It is funny how you sometimes don't see the things that are so great until you have another manager in your life who does everything the *wrong* way. I remember one of the managers I had after Frank had an amazing ability, one that I do not care to mirror. He would take credit for anything and everything that happened around him. Even if he was in the same city as something good that happened, completely unrelated to him, he would find a way to tie it back to himself and create a story as to how 'he" made it happen. If the Toronto Maple Leaf's won the Stanley Cup, this guy would take credit for it somehow. By having two complete polar opposites for a manager I was able to reflect and say, "Damn, Frank was *amazing* compared to this chump!"

Barry

What Happened

Barry was the guy who hired me for my first commission based mortgage sales job, which is still one of the business's I am in today. He was the best at forward-thinking. I remember when, in my second year in my commission-based mortgage role at the bank, I had the opportunity to do all the financing for a major condo project. There was over forty units, and I was going to have the opportunity to finance all of them. *Cha ching!* I had negotiated a marketing tool with the builder to do what was called an "interest rate buy down." This meant that in order to make the condos more marketable, the builder would buy down the interest rate for a three-year term in order to make the financing cost cheaper for the buyers. This was a slam dunk for me, as the builder would send anyone who was going to get a mortgage to me to do the deal. After about six months of hard work, closing day was approaching. I had completed financing for twenty-three units, I had all the paperwork prepared, and I met with the builder. I gave him the bill, which was approximately $250,000 in order to buy down all the interest rates for the mortgages that I had arranged. They looked back at me and said, "That's not right. We never agreed to this. That's your bill—not ours."

Whaaaaaaaaaaaaaaaat! My mouth hit the floor, and I believe about ten grey hairs came out of my head at that moment in time. I was speechless! I left that meeting wondering what my next career was going to be, because as far as I was concerned, I was *done* in the mortgage business. I immediately called Barry. I explained the trouble I was in, and how I was facing a potential lawsuit of over a quarter of a million dollars. He never once laid the blame game; as soon as I came to him, it was all about, "Okay, let's look at solutions." *Wow*—what a guy. He knew me and my values, and never once asked "Why did this happen?" He never once questioned my integrity or my actions. He went straight to "Okay Brian, here are the options we can look at." From there, we moved forward.

What I Made It Mean

You have to always be forward-thinking when adversity comes your way. I realized that the sooner I started to look for the solution, the sooner it would come! My advice to you is that instead of wallowing in the tombs of hell and getting overly depressed about what is going to happen, face the music and look for solutions ASAP. The sooner you look, the sooner they will appear, and the sooner you can move on.

Barry also taught me that when you are surrounded by good people, they will beat themselves up ten times more than you ever could (truth to that!). Help them get out of the jam, and don't make them dwell on it. Think of the solutions. When I had that lawsuit pending, he could have fired me, screamed and yelled at me, or reprimanded me, but all he did was say to me, "Okay, let's look at our options." What a breath of fresh air! I thought my career was over, and here was a guy who went straight to the solution.

By doing that for me, Barry made me fiercely loyal to him. This type of loyalty in any business is a must. Jim Collins, in his book From Good to Great, said "you need to have the right people on the bus" By having this fierce loyalty with a co worker, manager, or even staff member you can do any type of business with them and know they have your back. That is the type of person you want on your bus. You know they will always have your best interest at heart, and will do anything to make you successful. This loyalty is a common thread I find among great leaders and mentors, Frank was the same way. Loyalty creates leverage for your vision. When you have such loyal people you are able to grow your business exponentially. I constantly try and re create this loyalty in my day to day interactions with my team. I would have worked for Barry forever, had he not been moved to another district.

What To Do

Be the person that moves forward and not the one who dwells on the past when you have your own business. Surround yourself with good people, and when mistakes happen—*and they will*—find the solution. Don't focus on the mistake. If you are reading this and have the goals and ambition that I believe you do, you will find yourself in a position of leadership and influence in time (if you are not already). How well you handle these situations is what will earn you the respect to not only have tough decisions brought to you, but also the confidence that your people will bring you the problems that you want to hear about. This will install a truckload of loyalty for you, as well as for your customers, co-workers, employees, and anyone around you. Loyalty in this day and age is not bought; it's only earned over a long period of time and through tough situations.

John M.

What Happened

John, another one of my mentors, introduced me to my first network marketing business, and he told me about how to read and listen. "Readers are leaders," he used to tell me all the time. So I started reading and listening to any CD on how to improve my time management or leadership and sales skills. I always get an inspirational book before I get on a plane; it's now part of my routine whenever I go on vacation with my wife. In fact, she will affectionately remind me, "Hey babe, did you get your how-to-be-a-better-person book yet?"

As part of the network marketing business—which I will explore in great detail when we talk about being courageous—part of the program was to be enrolled in their "standing order system." This was $200 per month, and each month they would give me a book and two CDs on different business tools, such as closing techniques, objection handling, time management and most importantly, how to handle rejection (which I sure did get a lot of in the toilet paper business). I also have to mention that $200 a month was *a lot* of money for me. When John first told me I had to spend $200 per month, I had just purchased my first house, and was making $30,000 per year. John encouraged me and drilled into me that the best money you will ever spend is the money you spend on learning and making yourself a better person, as it will have huge returns. John was right.

What I Made It Mean

It is important to invest in yourself; even when you think you do not have the money, self-improvement is money well spent. I learned that there is a lot of negativity in the world, with people telling you that your goals will never happen, or that you're a big dreamer, or, "Good luck with that, bro!" I learned that filling your brain with positivity every day is no different than taking a shower every morning to clean the dirt off of you. The money you spend on yourself will pay you for years. You will *always* find a way to pay for things; it is just a matter of *what* you are choosing to pay for. I had to make sacrifices in order to afford those CDs; homebrewed beer and smokes from the reserve (unfortunately, I was a smoker for a long time, but I've quit now and I save money) were just a few things that I made sure to sacrifice on.

Never stop investing in yourself. Even to this day, I pay a coach on how to better manage my businesses. Just when you think you have arrived, make sure you check yourself, as there is still a better way to do things.

What To Do

Invest in yourself! Make sure that you listen to at least two educational audio programs, such as Tedtalks or Podcasts every week from someone who can teach you something—someone who will bring you up, and not put you down. Also ensure that you read a book every month. We have list of books on our Mission 35 website that are all amazing books to read. Your mentors can be the ones you read about and listen to. I love to read the LinkedIn Influencers on positive thinking each morning as soon as I get up. It starts my day on the right foot, and it gets me thinking the right way instead of watching the morning news about who died, the latest sports stats, or who screwed over who. Make sure you read for fifteen minutes before you go to bed every night; By sitting in front of the TV until you can't keep your eyes open, you will actually fall asleep in a worse mood. By feeding your mind before bed, you will reduce your stress level, enhance your sleep, increase your memory power and your vocabulary. Read a book!

Peter Hogben

What Happened

Peter Hogben: my Dad, the best mentor of all. As I mentioned before, my dad had the best attitude going. He demonstrated this perfectly in a home video he took one time. I was in my late teens when he got his first video camera, boy, did he like taping family vacations and holidays. He would never video tape himself, (he was not into the selfies) but you could always hear his voice. He was the constant narration of everything that was being videotaped, and it was always said with a smile in his voice. No matter what was being filmed, when you heard his voice it was as if it was the best thing happening to him in the world at that moment. Nothing could go wrong through his eyes. What seemed to be a painful annoyance as a trying to be cool teenager at the time, has turned out to be one my favourite things; now that he is gone. The way he filmed our family's memories is an amazing insight into his head and how he thought. One video was of me when I first got a sports car, and I was taking my brother for a ride. My brother was in a rocky relationship at the time, and when we got back from the joy ride, my dad was videotaping and hamming it up with the two of us in the driveway at the front of the house. He followed us into the backyard, where the rest of the family was. We were sharing the details of the thrill ride I had just taken my brother on to the rest of the family when my brother's long time girlfriend started giving him a hard time about not bringing her with him. As soon as the conversation became negative, my dad took the camera, slowly panned over his garden, and went off on a three-minute story about how nice the six-foot tall sunflowers were; he completely tuned out from what he saw as an unnecessary, unproductive, and negative conversation. It is amazing to re-watch this footage, as I remember the fight my brother got into; however, the memory that was caught on camera is actually a very funny one, that tells a completely different story.

What I Made It Mean

My dad taught me to sneak up on someone while at work or at home and discover something good that they are doing, as anyone can point out something wrong. He taught me not to have an ear for bullshit, and focus instead on the important things in life, such as making new memories. "Don't sweat the small stuff" is a saying that he really took to heart, and now I do, too. He also taught me unconditional love. Being a father myself has really ingrained in me what is important. Make sure you know what your values are, and stick to them. It's amazing the impact your positive values can have years later, just as my dad's did in his videos.

What To Do

Embrace the people you love in your life and be the example for them. When negative things come up, if you're going to have an ear for it, make sure it's a constructive one and not a destructive one. When people start gossiping to me—whether they are co-workers, customers, or employees— I have a thirty-second rule. If it goes on for longer than thirty seconds, I cut it off. This can be done by simply changing the subject, or my personal favourite, leaving the room. When someone is in my office and the conversation starts going this way, I have been known to just stand up and start walking towards the door. You would be amazed at how conditioned people are to just follow suit when you do something like this. Try it sometime; it is actually hilarious to watch. If you stand up in your office in the middle of a conversation and start walking towards the door, the person you are talking to will most often start following you unconsciously.

The more you tune out gossip, the less people will come to you and complain about things. You will gain a reputation for not having an ear for bullshit and looking for the good! This reputation gives you the time to focus on what is most important to you.

Chapter 3:
Be Courageous

Being courageous leads to growth.

"Courage is doing what you are afraid to do.
There can be no courage unless you are scared."
—Eddie Rickenbacker

When you are young, you have the absolute best opportunity of your life: you can 100% fuck up, and still have a place to live! I mean seriously, the only time in life that you do not have a husband or a wife, kids to feed, a mortgage to pay, and other crazy responsibilities is when you are young. When you graduate from university or college, or even when you leave high school and are trying to find yourself, the first thing most people do is either get a job right away or travel. Now, I have no problems with those who travel; however, for the ones who go out and get a job right away, I wager that is the *safest* thing you could do. As they say, nothing great ever comes without taking some risks. Start a business, try a 100% commission-based job, open a damn lemonade stand for goodness' sake!

Most people are fortunate enough to have a roof over their head and at least one loved one to take care of them when they graduate from post-secondary school. This is the time to take the risk; this is the time when you can recover from a colossal failure. If you try out a business, a commission-based job, or even a network marketing company, you will have just gained another degree in life, even if you fail. The beautiful part is that you will have truly lost *nothing* except for some time. What you will have gained in experience will far outweigh the time and energy spent.

And guess what? On the flipside, you could be wildly successful at a young age. How would that be? When you are married or have kids, you will have additional responsibilities; there will be other lives to take into consideration other than your own. This means that it will be much harder to go all in, but it won't be impossible. You can still start a part-time business—which, if you haven't already, do it now! There are amazing tax advantages to having a home-based business. No matter what it is, just pick something you like and do it. Don't listen to that little voice in your head that says, "That's stupid"—just do it (Nike is on to something). If you have a mortgage and a car payment, you really need to plan. Starting out with a part time small business is a great way to stick your feet in the water to gauge the temperature. Part time may be all you can do to start, depending on your circumstances. By sticking to the budgeting that we had discussed in chapter 1 you can save up 3 to 6 months of expenses if you are going to take the dive into a new business with less guaranteed income and more variable pay. *A strict budget will allow you* to go without income for three to six months. When you have a lot of financial obligations it requires more effort to make a change because you have to go further outside of your comfort zone, *and* it becomes easier to justify to yourself that, "Nah, things are just fine, it would be too hard to try and do something new." However, this assumption is entirely untrue.

What Happened

One of my best growing experiences was when I started my first company, which we called "Typants." I was on my way to study International Management in Sydney, Australia, and party my face off, when we stopped over in Thailand. We had stumbled across these pants, which at the time resembled hospital pants. They were a big fad at the time. I purchased about ten pairs of these paints while on Khao San Road in Bangkok, and I wore them everywhere. They had a fifty-two-inch waist (hold on—I wasn't *that* fat at the time), and had two drawstrings on the back, which tied around the waist. They were *sooo* comfortable, and at the time I thought they were pretty cool! After Thailand, I was on my way to Sydney with my new pants, and of course, they were a staple in my wardrobe. People were always asking me, "Hey, where did you get those cool pants?"

I started to think, *Why not market these things back home in Canada?* I called my best friend back home and pitched the idea to him. I think he may have been high at the time, but he said, "Let's turn this into a clothing empire—I'm totally in!" Everyone else back home who I shared the idea with thought I was crazy (or told me that at the very best, I had an amazing maternity wear clothing line). This was my first real dose of the naysayers in the world who were just trying to shoot me down. They didn't see my vision, share my excitement, nor think it was possible to do something like be an international fashion mogul. I was so pumped about the idea that I didn't listen to the negativity one bit; I was poised to be successful—and university-educated, I might add! What could go wrong?

When I returned home from my university adventure, we immediately got to work on the Typants empire. I was going to make millions off this idea, and you could not have told me anything different. We first thought of importing these pants from overseas, but when I got into researching it, it was *way* more money than I had available (raising funds for investment wasn't even in my vocabulary at this time). At the time, I knew that those who I surrounded myself with—my friends and family—were not the type of people who could educate me on how to pitch the idea and raise money to pursue my dream. That is why it is so important to surround yourself with people who have big ideas and big dreams just like you. Had I known then what I know now, I would have been able to reach out to a different network of people and raise capital for my venture. I would have been able scale my business quicker to more people. I would have been able to get more pants for a cheaper price.

I was still in the mentality of, "If it's meant to be, it's up to me." I had $4562.00 to my name, which was my life savings in my Registered Retirement Savings Plan at the time. Part of my dad's philosophy was to *always* pay yourself first, which I still do to this day. This was money—$50 a week—that I had been saving up while I was working my part-time job as a cashier at a local pet food store when I was in high school. I had been making about $8 an hour, I might add! It didn't pay that well, but I sure did learn a lot about what makes your dog's coat look shiny.

As I returned home from University in Australia in December, essentially staying out of country for 11.5 of the 12 months, my income in Canada was zero dollars that year. Seeing as my Dad taught me all about Registered Retirement Savings Plans I knew I was able to take the money out of my RRSP tax-free. This was knowledge my Dad had given me but I am quite sure not with this intention. *Wow, what a deal,* I thought to myself. When I told my dad about how smart I was with this idea that he had technically given me, he didn't share the same excitement. "That money is for your *retirement!*" he told me. "You better not take that money out, as it took you two years to save that money up!"

Well, of course, being twenty-two years old and knowing everything at the time, I didn't listen to him, and I cashed out. Besides, this $4,562 was going to turn into a million dollars in no time. I immediately took the money, found a local manufacturer in Mississauga, Ontario, and spent $5,000 on my first order of pants. I received five hundred pairs of pants— all black—and my business partner Jeff and I were ready to sell. All my friends and family purchased a pair; I'm pretty sure they did this out of charity, but nonetheless, their support was appreciated.

The first step was approaching the beach stores. We went to Sauble Beach, Wasaga Beach, and Port Dover and pitched our hearts out, and we eventually got into stores in each of these three beach towns. We even had the great idea of going back to the beach stores with our friends a week later, and giving them the money to buy our own pants! We thought, *This will show them what a hot product our pants are, and they will be dying to order more.*

Next were the local campus stores for Mohawk College and McMaster University. I thought that since I was such a hit in Australia, as all the girls would complement me on my cool pants, and all the "blokes" would ask me how they could get a pair, the same would happen here. Frosh week came and we bribed some hot girls with free pants to help us pitch the pants to new university students. The pants were a hit! By "a hit," I think we sold approximately twenty pairs of pants during the frosh week, but my sheer optimism told me that this was a huge deal. We were about a month in after receiving our first shipment of pants, and we had sold just shy of a hundred pairs of them. They had a wholesale price of $20, and were retailing for $40. I thought that we were well on our way. We had started doing bootleg commercials and grassroots marketing, and we were having so much fun doing it! I would sometimes think to myself that this was going to change my life. I remember some friends were asking me how it was going around this time, and my answer was, "I think we should hit about a million in sales next year." Apparently, my sales forecasting needed a bit of work at the time.

This all changed after a harmless game of golf with my good friends. One of them was playing in his Typants, which I think he wore around me just to make me happy (kind of like the sweater your grandma gave you, which you only pull out when she comes over for dinner). Anywho, at one point, my friend went to grab his ball, which was on the other side of a small stream. He jumped across, and as he did, I heard the distinct *riiiiiiiiip* sound. I instantly knew what it was, and my hopes and dreams started to crumble before my eyes. When he landed on the other side, he looked down and said, "What was that?" As he looked down, we were all able to see a gigantic, gaping hole in his crotch. That's right—the entire crotch had ripped from front to back, revealing some nice tighty-whiteys.

Of all the things to happen to my pants, the crotch had to rip. As it turned out, there was a design malfunction in how the pants were sewn together. More and more calls started to come in about these crotchless pants. Apparently, they were just fine if you just sat around and didn't do anything, but as soon as you started to move around in any athletic manner—*riiiiip*! It didn't help that our tag line for the pants was "More baggage for your junk"—turns out that there was no baggage at all. I thought to myself, *How could there be a design problem in these pants?* It then dawned on me. *I know why*, I said to myself. *It's because I know nothing about clothes!*

After that—which I affectionately refer to as the "worst golf game of my life," and was probably the reason why I hate the sport now—the calls started to pour in. "Mr. Hogben," they would say, "our pants seemed to have a rip in them." I even had to change dentist offices, as my mom told the dental office about my new adventure and the whole staff agreed to buy them as their new uniform. I was so embarrassed to show my face around there in case they had already ripped on the staff—or worse yet, be there when one of the pants ripped! The only logical thing to me at that age was to never go back to that dental office again. I had to change to another dental office and start fresh—that, and I had no money to refund all the pants. In hindsight, my parents probably paid them back without me even knowing.

This design flaw immediately tarnished the Typants integrity and the brand name (that is, what little brand recognition we had). My RRSPS were zero—and my credibility was shot, as I didn't have any money to refund people with—*but* I still had four hundred pairs of pants, which are still in my garage to this day.

What I Made It Mean

The "Typants era," as I fondly refer to it, gave me a lot of insight into the business world. I learned about preparation, follow-up, and rejection. I also learned that along the journey of your different business adventures, you will find people who will be your supporters and your cheerleaders—that is, those people who want to see you do well. When someone supports you, hang on to that person.

I learned many lessons from this experience that I brought forth in my next ventures and careers. I have never looked back at Typants as a failure, but instead as a colossal learning experience. The worst thing that could have happened would have been to listen to *all* my friends who had said, "I told you so." I could have taken that as a reason to never try anything different for fear that it wouldn't work out. I could have decided at that moment that I would never again step outside of the box.

Instead, I thought about how much money people spend on school and education, and for me to spend $4,562 (as well as a lot of my leisure hours) on this project was, in my mind, an MBA in itself. It had absolutely been the best time in my life for something like that to happen. I realized that I wasn't going to be a millionaire by the time I was twenty-five, but I also knew that deep down inside, I was one step closer to becoming a millionaire and achieving my dreams. To learn about how naive I had been in thinking that the path to success (and achieving my Mission of financial security at age thirty-five) would have come easy was the most valuable lesson I received at that time. When things don't work out, you need to pick yourself up. In actuality, one of the biggest challenges would have been being successful the very first time! Then you think you know it all, and the stakes are even bigger when you make another bonehead decision. Learning, trying, and especially crashing and burning on your first business venture is truly a blessing in disguise. So, hurry up and get on with it!

In having all of your life savings on the line, you are going to pay attention to the outcome; so it's better to put life savings that are under $5,000—rather than $5 million—all on one venture! Of course, at that age, I still had lots of time to recover from this devastating blow. The fact of the matter is that every time I have overcome fear in a major decision in my life, I have been able to grow my confidence.

What To Do

Be bold and start young. Do not be afraid to try something, because when you are young, you have *lots* of time to recover! Another thing to be sure of is, if one person says you're crazy, ask someone else. If the second person *also* says you're crazy, ask a third. If the third one says you're crazy, *go for it!* It means you're on the right track.

The reality is that only one person supported my Typants idea. When I made that call from Sydney Australilia back home to my best friend Jeff, he was the one on the other end of the phone saying "hell yah, I'll help you start a business, that's a great idea!" The flaw wasn't in the idea, but in the execution of it. I didn't put enough time and effort into the design process. The reason I knew it was a good idea is that this past year, I saw a girl pitch *my* pants on the television show Dragon's Den. The show where multi millionaire entrepreneurs invest in different business ideas. They had a different name, but one of the Dragons invested in them. *Damn!* They went on to have a million-dollar clothing company with my pants. Having the "right" partners can be a key to any business, which is a lesson I didn't learn until much later. This is not to say my friend Jeff was the wrong one to partner with, it just means that we were lacking in certain skill sets in order to not only design the pants correctly but also get them out to market. By having a different partner, such as one on Dragons Den, they will have knowledge and resources that you do not have which will allow you to more access. In our case this could have been access to online retailers, designer outlets, and so on. Don't be afraid to have more than one partner in a business. Get the right people and do not be afraid of or hide from your weaknesses. If you don't know something and do not have enough money to hire someone who does, you can always give up equity in your business. This can be a cheaper upfront model to gain the right people, but can cost you more in the end. So, once again, don't make the same mistakes I did, you may have an idea that a multi millionaire is just waiting to give you money for!

Get out and try something, *now!* Do some research, spend some time thinking about what you like and what you are passionate about, and do it! Do not spend all of your time planning the idea and execution of it, as you will get what is called "paralysis by analysis." You will think about it forever, and before you know it, the idea, the timing, and your energy will be all gone. Now, depending on what your current situation is, I am not saying throw caution to the wind, pull a Hail Mary, and hope to god it all works out. What I am saying is research a network marketing company. On the Mission 35 website, you can see that there are hundreds of different types of careers you can try that are commission-based or profit-driven where *you* are in charge of your income potential and your destiny. If nothing else, join a network marketing company. If you earn a salary as an employee for a company, there are huge tax advantages for being self-employed. Finding a business that is low in entry fees and start-up capital is tough, so a network marketing company is just your ticket. If you were to start you own business it could cost you 100s of thousands of dollars. You may need an office space, office equipment, staff, inventory and much much more! Typically in a network marketing company you would have a small start up fee, like $500 or $1000 as you do not hold onto any inventory, if you do its very little. You will not have to pay for massive advertising budgets, nor do you need to go and hire additional support staff, and the training is done by the person who recruited you. BAM you have a small business in no time with little money invested. By having your own small business you are able to write off expenses that most people use everyday such as you cell phone, gas for your car, and other small household expenses. Essentially keeping more of your hard earned money in your pocket. More on this later.

Later on, we will talk about real estate, and if you do not own a house now, *buy one!* You are never too young to start your empire; find a way to do it, especially if you are in post-secondary school, and *stop* listening to the reasons why you cannot do it, or the belief that you are too young. You will find that if you ask yourself the right question, your brain is an amazing tool, and it *will* find the answers for you, so long as you feed it the right program to start.

If you are fortunate enough to come from a family of affluence, look at the different businesses that can work for you instead of having *you* work for them. Make sure you try it now—I cannot stress this enough. The recovery is much easier when you are young rather than when you are older, and not to mention, your ego gets bigger the older you get, so you will think you already know everything. Have you ever met someone older than you that has all the answers, but none of the results that you would want to leave with? I run into these people all the time as they have been in the same job or industry for 10 or 20 years, and know exactly how it all works. These are the people I affectionately refer to as having 1 year experience 10 times. I ran into many of these people at an old mortgage office I worked for. They stopped learning after 1 year and just continued to repeat the same behaviour over and over and over again. They lost the courage to continue to learn and because of that stated a downward spiral in their business. By having courage you will continue to grow and succeed. Even when things don't work out, if you take what you learned and apply it moving forward, you have not lost anything, but will have gained an edge for the next business.

Chapter 4:
Buy Real Estate Now

Buying real estate = future financial freedom.

Don't wait to buy real estate; buy real estate and *wait!*
—*T. Harv Eker*

All the richest and wealthiest people in the world own *and* invest in real estate. From the beginning of time to the end of time, people will always have to live somewhere. This is not rocket science! I am not saying it is the be all and end all to build wealth; however, it should be something that you start *now*. The younger you are when you get into ownership, the better off you will be later on in life. There will be ups and downs, however, and I am not talking about timing the market; I am talking about buying property and holding onto it for a long time, as the longer you hold onto it, the price *will* go up, and the mortgage you have on it *will* go down.

Even if you are twenty years old, you should be looking at how to get your first house now. A lot of people have the notion that it will "tie me down," but this is *bullshit*! A house is not a noose around your neck; it is more like a helium-filled balloon that will help bring you up. *What if I get relocated to another city?* you may be thinking. *I will have to sell. I won't be able to take the job I really want, and I can never move once I have a property!* Stop that little voice, rent out the property, and make sure that it *pays* you every month. Positive cashflow should be part of your decision when you are purchasing to ensure that what you purchase has the ability to have a renter cover your expenses, even *if* you aren't living there.

If you want to find a reason to not buy a house, I *guarantee* that you will find one. You can justify everything and anything; for example: "The prices are too high right now," "Interest rates are too high," "The market is going to crash soon," "I can't afford one right now," or "I am not sure where I will be a year from now." If prices are too high in your area, then go outside your area. There is no rule that says your first house has to be the one you live in, so why not make your first house a rental property and start your portfolio now? In my hometown, we are in a serious boom; lots of first-time investors are purchasing outside of the city limits in the neighbouring areas, where the prices have not yet gotten out of control. Find a reason, and find a way.

Many people have told me in the past that they don't have any money to buy a house. Well, start asking for some. Ask your parents or family for money, and offer them a rate of return on the down payment they lend you. Most of you will have family who will have no problem giving their money to complete strangers at the bank, who will pay them 2-3% on their money. Why would your family not trust you with the money? And also, offer them double the return. When my dad loaned me the $5,000, I offered him a 6% return on his money, which was double what his conservative Canada Savings Bonds were paying him. I have heard many people say, "I want to do it all on my own, and I don't want any help from my parents." This is where pride kicks in for some people, which I will always ask, how much extra are you willing to pay for you pride or ego? A complete stranger can lend you the money as well, but this will be ten times more expensive than if you asked your family. Do you still want to do it on your own? Make your goals bigger than your ego, as most times, the ego is getting in the way of your goals.

Find a consignor or a business partner to venture with. Maybe your family doesn't have any money, either; in this case, if you have found some mentors along the way and have really tapped into them, ask them for resources, money, or other people to joint venture with on a real estate deal. You will likely get some "Nos" along the way, but don't let that stop you! Every "No" you get is one step closer to a "Yes." If I stopped after my first hundred "Nos," I would still be selling pet food at my first job (but I would be damn good at it)! There is *always* a way to purchase real estate; you need a great mortgage broker (nudge, nudge) and a plan.

In my short life thus far, I have yet to find one person who purchased real estate and held onto it for at least ten years who has regrets. The right time to purchase something is *now*. Stop the excuses, and make it happen.

What Happened

I remember buying my first house. I was on the look out for a duplex. I needed to have rental income in order to survive. I had been back from Australia for a year, and it was during the time when I was working my ass off for the thankless promotion I was soon to get. I really had to budget myself, as on my $30,000 gross income, I could not afford much—and not to mention the fact that all my savings went up in pants! My RRSPs were gone, and being a single guy at the time, even though I was living at home, it wasn't easy to save up money. Also, I still owed my parents approximately $29,000, as they had taken out a secured line of credit in order to help me go to university in Australia. That money was easy to spend at the time, but paying back $200 every two weeks when I was back home made it feel like I was going *nowhere*; it seemed like it was never going to get paid off. So I thought to myself, *I can either stay at home and keep paying back my student loan* (which would mean I would still be living in my parent's house at thirty-five!), *or I can come to terms that I will always have some debt, but it is important to start growing my assets, as well.* This was a tough sell to my parents—at least I think it was; in hindsight, they were probably quite excited at the thought of finally being empty nesters, as my brother had just moved out as well, not too long ago.

I had approximately $2,500 in savings, I was twenty-three years old, and the idea of buying a house scared the shit out of me! *What if I cannot pay for it?* I worried. *What if the roof leaks? What if I don't get a renter? What if I get fired? What if, what if, what if?* If I had listened to all the crazy talk (that is, negative self-talk) in my head, I never would have done anything. I decided I would make it work. *No matter what, I will make it work—I am smart and resilient, and I know my parents will help me out if push comes to shove*, I told myself.

I looked for months, and I finally found what I thought was the perfect place. It was actually a dump when I moved in, with old piss-stained carpets, an ugly, dated kitchen, a deck that was falling apart, windows that didn't even open, and creaky floors. But to me, it looked like home sweet home. To give you an idea of how bad a shape this place was in, I had lived there for over two months when my dad came over to help me seal off some of the drafts using plastic wrap over the windows (yup, you heard me), because I had been complaining that the house just didn't get warm; however, we discovered a basement walkout door that couldn't fully close! It was a quarter of the way open because the frame was warped, and cold, winter air was pouring in. This house was so brutal that I hadn't even realized that the basement door was half open for *two months!*

Regardless of the decrepit shape it was in, it was a duplex, and I knew I could rent out the upstairs for $850 a month. The cost of it was $160,000. This happened in December of 2003 a time when I was able to buy the house with a zero down payment. However, the interest rate was 6.75%. Writing this right now as a mortgage broker floors me, as I am currently lending our private mortgage loans at this interest rate! And for you nay-sayers out there stay tuned as I will show you how this scenario still works in todays market, with much higher prices. Anyhoo, I calculated that my mortgage payment was going to be $1,040 a month. I thought this meant that I would only have to pay $200 a month for living on my own, plus property taxes and utilities. The property taxes with the heat and hydro added up to another $500 a month. I could live on my own, pay down a mortgage, and own a property for $700 a month. So get this straight, I had expenses of $1540 a month, and I was receiving rent of $850 a month. That is $700 a month out of my pocket, not bad! I could have rented a shitty apartment for the same amount back then, but instead I was owning. I would still pay my parents a reduced amount of $150 per week and have some money left over to go out drinking. Mind you, I did have to start brewing my own beer for a couple of years, as this was much cheaper than supporting my local liquor store. I purchased the house and moved in December of 2003.

What I Made It Mean

That first house was a real milestone. I experienced such an emotional fear of, "Am I really responsible enough to do this? Can I really afford my own house?" It was extremely stressful for about two weeks, while I was getting my financing approved, doing the home inspection, and meeting with the lawyer. However, after those two weeks and when all the bills had rolled in after forty-five days, I realized that my numbers were right (give or take $50). The planning had really payed off. A *huge* sense of confidence come over me when I thought, *I am twenty-three years old and I own my first house! Damn right! I rock! I can do anything—I am the man!* All the little fears disappeared; there was no way that I would not make ends meet—I would do dishes if I had to in order to make things work, because I was a homeowner, and I wasn't about to ever lose my house.

I remember having my first BBQ a couple of months later. I was all by myself, cooking some burgers in my backyard (on the dilapidated deck) drinking a beer (a homebrew, of course), smoking a cigarette (Native smokes), and thinking to myself, *I did it!* I was reflecting on all those great emotions that home-ownership brings: *I am the man, I bought a house, and I did it all on my own, way to go, Bri!* It was at this time when a different reality started to set in. I said to myself, "Wow, you just got a twenty-five-year mortgage, all of your money is spoken for, and if you don't plan on living in a duplex forever, eating no-name burgers and drinking home-brewed beer on a shitty waiting-for-a-lawsuit back deck, you have to do something more." I had finally achieved success in my eyes by moving out of my parents basement and purchasing my first house! Then it was time to go back to the drawing board.

What To Do

If you are renting now, stop right there and make yourself a plan to purchase a house. Talk to a mortgage broker, and see how you can get pre-approved for a mortgage. If you can't get pre-approved for a conventional mortgage, make a strategy and develop a business plan for how you can borrow money from a friend or a family member in order to get yourself into a house. See a Mission 35 Mortgage Broker, and they will help you find a solution and make a plan for you (www.mission35.com). In addition, check out our first home investment plan.

Now you may be thinking to yourself, this will not work for me, as house prices are so much more expensive now and I can not get into the market. I want to show you the same example I used on my first house in todays dollars. As when I sold the house over 10 years later, it was worth $450,000. Not a bad increase from the $160,000 I purchased it for. When I sold the house, the rents were significantly different from when I purchased it. The 3 bedroom unit on the top floor could be rented out for $1600 per month, a nice increase from the $850 per month when I purchased it. The mortgage payment on a house like this with 5% down is approx. $2079 per month with taxes and utilities you are looking at another $800 per month. That would make your total monthly costs to own the home $2879. If you MINUS the rental income you are receiving, of $1600 per month, you could be living in your own home for $1200 per month. This is the same as renting a nice apartment. The difference today, from when I purchased is that there are no longer 0 down payment mortgages. You will have to find 5% in order to make the down payment. Find a way to get the funds, as we discussed there are joint ventures, family investment, and partnerships. Keep asking until you get a "Yes" from someone. Take note that as I write this in 2017 interest rates are more on your side than they were for me. You can still get a mortgage today for under 3% where I was paying almost 7%. Don't let yourself fall in the excuse trap. This is where you keep justifying, rationalizing, or make excuses as to why you can not do something. The only limitation is you, and how hard you are willing to try, and how much you will step out of your comfort zone in order to get to your financial security.

There is no reason you should be renting. I don't care if your credit is terrible, or if you have a *ton* of debt. Maybe you have to take a step back and declare bankruptcy before you take a step forward. I don't know your situation. However, I do know that with determination and a desire to succeed, you can get a house. It may not be the house you want right now, however; you have to work to get to that. The first house may be in a terrible location that you hate, but you have to pay the price in order to get where you want to go.

Another thing to consider is that if you do have a duplex or a property that you rent out a portion of, you have some *major* tax savings in Canada. You are able to write off a portion of your interest on the mortgage, utilities, house insurance, and even repairs. This is a massive benefit in helping you reduce taxes (which are the biggest expense you will ever have!). Make sure that you get a great accountant to help you navigate this process. Money spent on an accountant is money well spent. I love my current accountant, as his knowledge has helped me save *tons* of money.

Lastly, don't get too hung up on your own success for too long. I know some people who never take the next step, because they have achieved home-ownership, and for some that is more than what they thought they would ever get. Enjoy the win and celebrate it (we will talk more about this later), but be sure to get over yourself, as well. If you keep on singing your own praises for too long, you will never move forward and achieve your Mission.

Chapter 5:
Work Hard and
Condense Your Career

"Hard work beats talent when talent doesn't work hard."
—Tim Notke

There are 168 hours in a week. Most people work at a job for at least forty hours of each week, and sometimes even up to fifty hours in that week, if you are working overtime and whatnot. Now, let's say you sleep an average of fifty-six hours a week (if you think that is not enough, that's eight hours a night, Sleeping Beauty!). Of course, you have to eat and have some social and family time; let's call that another four hours per day. If you add all of this up, it equals around 124 to 134 hours per week. You know how much that leaves you? 34 to 44 hours per week. That is enough time for another job!

You have enough time in your week to work another job, and you are wondering where all the time goes. The average person spends four hours a day watching TV! That is over twenty-eight hours a week (if you are average), I hope this is one category you are *not* above average in. Depending on your poison, the stats for social media are over four hours a day. To put that into perspective, that is over 1.5 *years* in the next ten years of your life! Now, don't sit there and try and figure out how this is wrong, or else you will have already missed the point. No matter what you have to say, I will go toe-to-toe with you and argue that you *do* have enough time in order to work a second job.

However, that is not my point. Do not work a second job, as that will just frustrate you and get you nowhere faster. My point is to show you that you *do* have the time to commit to something else that will make you money. There is enough time in the day to work your full-time job, as well as learn about trading stocks, hedge funds, real estate investment, raising capital, network marketing, and all of those things. Stop watching the damn TV and stop creeping around on Instagram and Facebook. If you want to be able to reach your Mission, you need to work twice as hard in a shorter amount of time. Most people want to retire by the age of fifty-five, and they think they are doing pretty damn good! Well, if you want the "Mission35" plan, you have to cram *a lot* of years into a short period of time—and I wish I could tell you it is going to be easy, but it ain't! It is going to be hard, and it is going to test you. That is why we talked about health goals at the beginning of the book; because in order to get the most from your body, you better be sure you are fuelling it as best you can with exercise and proper nourishment. Otherwise, you are going to feel lazy—in both body *and* mind—and not do what is required to get you off the sofa and working.

What Happened

There was a time when—no word of lie—I thought I was on the edge of the cliff. I was working for the bank as a Personal Banking Officer; I was part of a network marketing company, making *no money* but spending $200 a month on an education program; I had two piece-of-shit rental properties that I couldn't afford unless they were rented out; and I was taking courses to increase my knowledge at the bank in order to get a promotion.

There was one night when I thought I had officially lost my marbles. I had a rental property where a tenant had moved out on the 30th, and so I had the one night to go into the property, clean it, paint it, and have it all ready for the next afternoon, when the next tenant would move in. I finished my last appointment, went home, had a quick bite to eat, got changed into my grubby clothes, and then went to get things taken care of. As soon as I got there, I got a phone call from a client who needed a big mortgage and needed to see me ASAP. *This would be great credibility for me if I get this deal*, I thought. *I may get a promotion!* It was only 6:00 p.m. at the time, so I figured I would go and see them at 7:30, then go home, get changed, and come back for 9:00 p.m. and just end up working till the wee hours of the morning to get it all done.

As soon as I hung up, I got another phone call from the tenant at the other property, freaking out that I had to get over there right now, as there was sewer water all over the floor; the plumbing had backed up in the basement apartment, and yup, the shit hit the fan! I immediately ran over there with a mop and started doing everything I could before the Roto-Rooter guys I had called (and could not afford, so I had to put them on credit) showed up to fix the problem.

I was knee-deep in rental property fun when my cell phone rang again; it was my clients who I was supposed to meet, asking me where I was. Oh *man!* I had forgotten about my appointment! I apologized profusely and lied through my teeth, saying I had had a family emergency—well, it was kind of a family emergency (for my tenants).

The Roto-Rooter guys finally showed up around 10:30 p.m. I had been mopping out crap for about three hours, and I was exhausted. I then realized I still had to go back to my other unit—which was a pigsty—and get it ready for the new people moving in. I worked till 4:30 in the morning, and then I went back home to sleep for a couple of hours before going back into work again for 8:30 a.m. Somebody shoot me!

It was at this time when John Mogford, one of mentors, said to me, "Brian, I know you feel like you are on the edge, but remember, the best fruit grows furthest out on the limb of a tree!" At the time, I think I would have preferred playing it safe and chewing some bark on the trunk of the tree! I was working 9:00-5:00 at my job and then studying for tests during the night for two to three hours; I was having a meeting once a week for the network marketing company; and I was trying to keep up with renos on the crappy rentals that I had purchased. I was easily putting in an eighty-hour workweek for almost two years. I still would make time once a week to go out with friends on a Friday or Saturday night and get absolutely drunk off my face—off of homebrewed beer and wine, of course. I told all of my friends that I didn't believe in hangovers; it was all just a state of mind. Meanwhile, I felt like absolute garbage when I woke up, and I would make myself go to the gym or for a run so that I could be mentally ready for all the things I had to do that day.

What I Made It Mean

This was when I realized and learned about the choices I was making. In order to achieve my Mission 35, feeling like I was working 2 full time jobs was part of the sacrifice I was going to have to make. I learned that there are multiple paths in life, and the one that most people typically take is the one that stretches out the working career to over forty years; so someone fully entering the workforce at age twenty-five would retire at sixty-five. If I were going to more than half that game plan, it would mean condensing things and adding pressure. There would be some sleepless nights, but being young and full of piss and vinegar, why not? What else was I going to do? As they say, that is how diamonds are formed: under an extreme amount of pressure. Choosing this path means having more on the go than the average Joe. My dad also taught me that if you want something done, give it to the busy person. During these years, I learned that when something needs to get done, you got to get it done in the time that you allotted for it. And if you cannot commit to something, then don't say that you will.

Having my time stretched to the max, really got me flexing my patience muscles, and the more you work a muscle, the stronger it gets. By realizing there is only so much time in the day, I had to learn how to leverage myself again. I turned this into a goal-setting exercise, in that if I wanted to grow my real estate portfolio, I needed to get to enough properties to have a property manager so that I could turn it into a business. Which I am happy to say I have today, as it would be impossible to grow without one.

The worst thing I could have done was listen to others at this time, who were saying, "Just sell the houses take the extra $50,000 you have made in profit and enjoy yourself. You work too hard—enjoy your life!" I really thought about this for a while, as that would have been the *easy* thing to do, but it would have really reduced my options later in life. People do not want you to do the hard things, nor do most people want to cheer you on when you are going against the grain. Most will tell you to do something only because it will make them feel better about what they are doing. When you are working harder than everyone else, people will say you work too much because they will feel guilty about not doing the things they *should* be doing in order to get themselves to where they really want to go. Don't sell out to the naysayers; it doesn't pay off.

What To Do

Those were some of my toughest years, and if I had to do it all over again I would. Being in my twenties with a bold goal and a Mission, I was determined to make it work. At that age, you have the time and energy to do it—so do it. As you get older your mind will make it harder on you, and your body if you don't take care of it. The older you are the stronger you need to make your vision in order to pull you through the struggling times. Don't make excuses for yourself. If you give your self a passionate enough reason, you will find a way to work that extra bit more. If you are struggling go back to your goals, and make sure it is something that inspires you and makes you grind out the extra hours.

Look at your current week and find out where you are wasting time. Document your hours from the time you get up until the time you go to bed for 7 days. Find out where you can enhance your day and get more done. I would wager that there is 2-3 hours a day, if not 5-8 hours on a weekend that you could be more purposeful with your time. Once you have identified this time for yourself, make a new schedule for yourself and give yourself hours for you new part time hustle. Clock in and clock out as if you were going to work, tell someone about it make them keep you accountable to it, that way you have to do it. Check out mission35education.com for a time blocking schedule.

If you are serious about your Mission, then you need to start getting serious with your time now. Never in my life have I said, "I don't have time" (ask my wife, and she might differ); however, the point is that you either *choose* to make time, or you *choose* not to. In either case, the choice is yours. How are you choosing to spend your time?

Chapter 6:
Invest Your Money, Don't Save Your Money

"An investment in knowledge pays the best interest."
—*Benjamin Franklin*

There will be so many temptations along the way that will encourage you to succumb to the "bigger, better, more" mentality. For example, a better, faster car that will help you pick up chicks (yup, that was me), or a better house where people will be impressed by how well you're doing. This is all *bullshit!* The material items don't matter as much as you think they do. The reality is that you will be far happier sticking to your Mission than you would be with the temporary gratification you'd get from borrowing more than you should to live in a house or drive a car that you think other people would be impressed by (*or* that you think you deserve). Get over yourself!

Living comfortably doesn't mean that you live like a bum—quite the contrary. It means spending your money in a way that is necessary and investing the rest. You will have all the time in the world after you hit your Mission date, to blow it all if you choose; however, I would wager that the freedom you will have provided for yourself—as well as the awareness of what is truly important—will be worth so much more than the flashy house or car. I have seen so many people—in my career, especially—who ask me, "How much can I afford?" By taking your extra money and investing it, you can actually see it grow and learn the power of leverage. By purchasing a piece of real estate, you will learn about *appreciation* instead of buying that cool car and learning about *depreciation*! Lots of people will tell you to *save* your money, and I am not advocating not saving. However, make sure that you do something proactive with your savings. Make it work for you; do not just let it sit there and hope that someone else is going to take care of you. No one else is going to take care of your financial future except for you.

The most popular tool that people gravitate towards when looking to invest is mutual funds. A mutual fund is a group of stocks put together, which in theory is supposed to reduce the risk. A stock for example is a share of ownership in a company. If you own a share of Bell, and the company does well, then you will make money on your share or stock. If the company does poorly, you will loos money on your stock. In a mutual fund you may own, Bell, Royal Bank, Google and many more all in one portfolio all for a relatively small cost. The entry fee into a mutual fund is quite low, usually as low as $1000 to $5000. The benefit is that you have shared the risk of your investment between numerous companies so if one goes down another may go up etc.

There are 2 problems that have arose in the mutual fund industry. The first one is the number of options that are out there, and the second one is the fees. Let's talk about options. As mutual fund companies can be very profitable more and more options have come up over the years, this has created a market where there are actually more combinations of stocks than there are the actual combinations of stocks that make them up! Meaning there are more combinations of the same thing than there are the very thing that makes it up! How does one choose in this massive array of choice? Investment advisors will have you fill out a questionnaire to determine your risk tolerance and than advise you as to which one to invest in. Now don't get me wrong there are some excellent investment advisors out there, ones that really know their stuff. I do recall when I was in my early 20's and started working at a bank, I was advising people with tens, sometimes hundreds of thousands of dollars where to put there money when I didn't have a pot to piss in nor a clue about what it actually meant, this should be a frightening thing for your financial future. Not to mention today they are talking about completely automating your investment with Robo advisors.! This means you would not even talk to a human being about your goals, a computer would make the decision for you based on the questions you answer. Well, I guess this is an option for you to leave your financial security up to Bob the Robot. Probably not the best option in my mind. The second issue is in the cost of these mutual funds and lack of accountability. Mutual funds have something called a MER or Management Expense Ratio. This is a cost for the fund manager to buy and sell the stocks that make up the fund. The idea is that they buy low and sell high in order to make bigger return on the mutual fund. These MERs can cost up to 3 or 4% per year. To put that into perspective, if the fund is saying that you make 6 or 7% in a year, be cautious as to weather that number is AFTER the fee or before. As if it is before, which in most cases it is, your actual return on your money could be only 3 or 4%. To add more fuel to the fire, the majority of mutual funds do not beat the market average. This means that when you invest your money someone is charging you to take care of it REGARDLESS of weather they even make you money. You still have to pay if you lose money, and most of them are less than average at what they do.

There is a low cost option which is often over looked and this is what is called an index fund. An index fund will simply follow the market, depending on the market you are in, such as the Toronto Stock Exchange, (TSE), or the Dow Jones Industrial Average (DJIA) These index funds are not actively managed, so you do not have to pay a high MER, instead you pay a nominal fee of often less than 1% in order to be in these types of funds. In my eyes you are getting the market performance, at a lower risk, which would technically net you a higher return in most cases.

Do not leave it in someone else's hands; as we mentioned before, you have 168 hours in a week, so learn about something you are interested in and how to invest your money. Learn about index funds, mutual funds, real estate and more. Once you learn about it put your money in it! Do get analysis paralysis, where you look at everything for so long and never make a decision. When you have your money on the line you WILL pay attention and make sure you understand what it is going on. Check out www.mission35.com for some ideas on what you can learn about.

What Happened

After that depressing episode on my poor excuse for a deck, I started to think, *How can I get my first rental property?* I did some research, and of course being in the banking world, I had some ideas on how I could get my next house. I realized that there was no way for me to buy a rental property with zero down, and I would, at the very least, need a 5% down payment. One of the reasons I was looking for rental properties was because I was reading a lot of Robert Kiyosaki at the time, with great books such as *Rich Dad Poor Dad* and *Cashflow Quadrant* (which I highly recommend you put on your reading list). But a rental property also made sense. If I moved back home and rented out my current place for $700 a month, I could actually be making a little bit of money! I know it wasn't a lot, but the principle to me was simple: how many houses do I need to own in order to replace my income? If I took home $2,000 net income a month (if I could find five houses that each generated $400 positive cash flow a month), I technically could retire from doing a job I *have* to do, and do what I *want* to do. What this did for my thinking at the time was give me options; and also, by thinking this way, my potential has grown exponentially and given me more options than what I had at twenty-three with only one fully leveraged house.

I found a property in a not-so-desirable location; I sure knew how to pick winners, but the cash flow was great! It had three units in it, and the rents were $450, $650, and $600, for a total of $1,700 per month. I was able to get this property for a purchase price of $120,000, and my mortgage payment on this would be $650 a month. My other expenses on the property were approximately $600 per month, including all the utilities, property taxes, and insurance; however, this left over $450 per month. Now, in order to get the down payments for this house, that is where my parents came into play. I put a business proposition together for them where I asked them to loan me $5,000 at a 6% interest rate, payable back to them in exactly twelve months' time (or $5300 from $5,000). As I mentioned at the beginning of the book, when I first told my dad, he said to me, "Why do you need two houses? You can only live in one at a time." Not to mention that I still owed him money for my school. My dad quickly picked up on the idea that once I had the $5,000 loan paid back, it would mean that I could pay back the student loan quicker as well, using the additional money that I would have coming in.

Now, I am sure lots of people have read about owning rental properties, and they think it's easy, but it's not! If someone tells you it's easy, that is a *lie!* If you want to make money in rentals, in my experience, you are purchasing less desirable properties in less desirable areas, which require more hands-on work. You typically get tenants that do not pay, do not keep the place clean, and so on. I would work my ass off at work and then have to go to a property at night—sometimes at 7:00 or 8:00 p.m.—and paint it, as someone had just moved out and left it in a terrible condition, and I wanted to show it to someone new the next day. I would be there till sometimes 3:00 or 4:00 in the morning, and then I'd have to get up for work at 8:00 a.m. again the next day.

This is partially what Mission35 is about; there was no magic wand or secret sauce that got me to where I am. I worked harder than a lot of people were willing to. I had to say "No" to *a lot* of cottage vacations with friends, in addition to some parties and other social events. I am not saying that I didn't have any fun at all, but you really have to be focused on what is important. You have to be so strict with your time, pick your friends accordingly, and make sure you are spending time with the people who truly add to your life and not the ones who are sucking it away from you.

This first rental was truly a springboard for me, as after that, I truly started to see the benefits of what can be done, and where I can go with this rental thing!

What I Made It Mean

Real estate was my ticket. It was the only tool I had found that could make me money while I was sleeping. It was the only tool that I saw the massive amount of leverage it could afford. If you have $20,000 in the bank and make 5% per year, at the end of the year you have earned $1000 of interest, OR a total of $21,000. If you take that same $20,000 and make a down payment on a house for $400,000 and the value of the house goes up by

5% (which is a VERY conservative appreciation for a house over time) the house would have grown to $420,000. This would mean that on paper your $20,000 would have increased your wealth by $20,000 essentially doubling your money! Not to mention that if you had a mortgage for the balance, you would pay off another $6000 of the principal on the loan, depending on the terms. This essentially makes the return on your investment 130%!! Your $20,000 has netted you a return of over $26,000. Now I know if you sold after a year there would be other costs to account for, but if you are already thinking that way you are missing the big picture. When you invest in a property it should be for the long term, do not be short sighted and look only 1 year out. You can see how this grows into the 100s of thousands of dollars in a short period of time!

By figuring out the power of leverage and real estate at a young age, I was able to really overcome my fear of debt. Getting debt to grow is a good thing. I mean, if the banks are able to take on billions of dollars worth of debt (the money you deposit with them) and lend it out again to make the spread (the difference between what they pay you for the deposit and what they lend it out to you at) why cant I do the same! By purchasing rental property, I knew after my 2nd one that it would exponentially grow my wealth while I was sleeping.

What To Do

Pick no more than 3 streams of income that you want to focus on and invest in. I have met people that own 20 different businesses at a young age and think they are well diversified. When you dig deeper and ask more questions they may only own 5 or 10% of a lot of companies, where they have no real influence on the business or actual knowledge on how it is performing or how to better the business. Crowd funding is very popular today (this is a way for businesses to build up capital, and in some cases, are giving away very small portions of the equity or ownership in the business) which is why you can see, or hear of people with lots of little pieces of big pies. A lot of people will tell you that diversity is the key, and I believe this to be bull shit! I invested in real estate by purchasing houses, my business which was also related to real estate was commission based mortgage sales, and lastly I was continually investing in myself. My ongoing commitment to life long learning. What did I learn about? More real estate! Diversity is when you are not sure what is happening in a certain industry, a lack of knowledge, and lastly when you have some serious wealth. When you actually hit your Mission, I would than look to diversify, into the 3 major asset categories, paper assets, real estate and business. However as you accumulate assets and knowledge it should be in an industry you like, are committed to learning more about and have a passion for. For me that was Real Estate. I still to this day think it is the easiest way to hit your Mission. There is no reason why you can not diversify your investment in one industry as well. Today I am able to make money in an up or down market in real estate based on the knowledge that I have acquired over the years. As you start to grow, more and more "shiny balls" will show up. You know the ones, the opportunities that come your way and say you can make a ton of money if you invest in this new stock that I just heard about, or this new company that I just heard is going to be huge. As the saying goes, easy come easy go. If you are not knowledgeable about an investment, don't make the investment. It is up to you to know what you are investing in and ensure you have the resources to make it successful. If someone has the "hot" stock you should invest in, remember how many people did it go through in order to get to you.

You should not get into speculative investments until you are at least 75-80% along the way to your Mission. Speculation in real estate is when you are buying strictly for the upside, meaning that there is no positive cashflow, (it is not paying you every month) and you are simply banking on the fact that it should be worth more later. This is a sure fire way to loose A LOT of your hard earned wealth. Yes, lots of people do this, but that does not mean you should, don't make me quote you the whole if s a guy jumps off a bridge speech!

Start with one stream of income that you want to invest in, from there see what will compliment it. Take Mcdonald's for example, why did they turn into a real estate company? Because they had so many locations that needed to lease. Why did they purchase a ketchup manufacturer? Because people like their ketchup and they go through a ton of that sugary red magic sauce that goes good on everything. Being in the real estate market, lead to being in mortgages for me. Being in the mortgage market lead me to private lending money for hard to place mortgages. All of these things were a natural progression and a compliment to the business that I was in. I was able to critically assess all of the upside risk and downside risk for each of these opportunities because of the day to day knowledge I was acquiring. Pick a stream, and start swimming. Invest money now.

Chapter 7:
Start a Business and Work for Yourself

"Build your own dreams,
or someone else will hire you to build theirs."
—Farrah Gray

Choosing a career that will allow you to grow and make your own destiny comes with a risk; however, it is actually less risky to start your own business or learn to sell than it is to work with another organization that can decide your fate regardless of your performance. I tired selling pants, for Pete's sake. What did I know about clothing, other than being in Thailand and seeing some cool pants? However, as I mentioned, Typants was a great lesson in following up and following through! No matter what you do, and what business you try, you will pave the way for your future greatness, the only way you will fail is by not getting up dusting yourself off and taking what you have learned and jumping into the next one!

The best reason to start a business, big or small is for taxes! No matter what it is, by having a business you have the ability to keep more of your hard-earned money. Take your cell phone, and car expense as an example. I think we can all agree that you will have or will need these 2 things at some point in your career. Now understand that if you pay for something with *after* tax dollars, instead of *pre tax* dollars that there is a major difference. *After* tax dollars, is the money you get from your job. You get a pay cheque and the money you receive is after taxes have been taken off. So if you have a salary of $60,000 per year. You will pay tax of approximately 20%

so your *after tax* income is $48,000. That is the money that goes in your pocket. From your $48,000 you then pay your cell phone bill, and your car expenses. These are *after* tax expenses. Let's assume your cell phone bill is $1200 for the year, and your car expense is $7200 for the year. ($400/month for a lease and $200/month for gas and insurance) After you pay taxes and these 2 expenses you are left with $39,600 for disposable income.

Now if you have a business, and you use your cell phone and your car for your business, which I believe is reasonable in most cases, you can pay for those expenses with *pre* tax income. Hence if you made $60,000 and then subtracted the expense above of $1200 and $7200, your income would reduce by $8400, making your income $51,600. Now you would only pay taxes on the $51,600. This would put you in a lower tax bracket, and reduce your taxes to approx. $8300. That means that with the same income and expenses as the salary person you are left with $43,300. That is a savings of $3700 in REAL DOLLARS! That is more money in your pocket with the exact same income and expenses. If you are able to save an extra $3700 per year, and even if you made NO money on your small business, but I bet you will, you could have the down payment saved up for your next rental property in 5 years. This is a very small example of how this can help you build your wealth. There are many more tax advantages, which include having a home office. If you have a home office you can reduce a portion of the interest on your mortgage, heat, hydro, property taxes, house insurance, even renovations! Now check with your accountant, as I said before this will be the best money you spend on professional advice. My accountant always told me the pig can get fat but the hog will get slaughtered. This means that if you are too greedy with Revenue Canada and try to cheat the system, they will catch you. However, there is no reason why you can not use these deductions to your advantage to help you grow your wealth! Remember to think of money in after tax dollars, and it will train your brain to think about how much you are actually keeping, instead of how much gross income you have.

What Happened

I remember my first year in commission-based selling; I worked for a major bank, selling mortgages. The Typants idea had gone up in flaming crotches, and I was now ready to tackle a new adventure. I had been working for a bank for several years, and I was in a financial planner role; "Personal Banking Officer" was what they called it. I had been passed up for the CEO position, which I thought I most definitely deserved, as I had gotten a university degree and a college diploma, in addition to getting my personal financial planning designation. In my naive mind I thought I knew everything. In reality, I had applied for a position that was two levels higher than mine, and I remember the hiring manager at the time telling me, "You are just not ready!" *Damn you,* I thought to myself, and considered finding out where he lived and egging his house. Apparently, my maturity level had not blossomed as much as my academic abilities.

Then I thought, *I will put my nose to the grindstone and work my ass off in my personal banking role.* That year, I had applied myself, worked extra hours, taken my work home, taken extra courses, and even dressed up as a stupid teddy bear for a fundraiser, where I walked around hugging young kids and old ladies; in short, I did everything I thought was required in order to get to the next stage and climb that corporate ladder. By the end of that year, I had far exceeded my targets, and I'd gotten an "Exceeds expectation" on my performance review. That meant a bonus of approximately $2,500, as well as a raise. At the same time, a spot opened up in my branch for a SR Personal Banking Officer; oh yay, baby, this was my ticket to the big time! I applied for the job, along with three other candidates. I went through the grueling interviews—and yes, I got the job! I thought, *This is amazing. I am one step closer to that CEO position. It will just be a matter of time.*

It was only a week later when reality finally hit me. It happened when I got my paycheque. I received, after taxes, an extra $20 biweekly on my pay. This was after my big promotion and getting double the work load in my new job. What the hell kind of reward was this for working my ass off? It was then that I realized that I couldn't work for someone else. The expression "If it's meant to be, it's up to me" crept into my head. I then realized that it was time to try out a more lucrative type of position. One where my earning potential was not capped based on the job level. This was when I jumped face first into commission based selling.

When I first started the commission role, I thought, *Wow, what freedom I have! I can make as much money as I want.* I was truly enamoured by the idea that if I made a lot of money, then I had myself to praise, and if I made no money, then I had myself to blame. The entire blame game was out of my vocabulary, and I was able to take full responsibility for my future now. But damn, I didn't realize it would be so hard! I can remember almost five times when I thought to myself, *I should just go teach English in Thailand. I can have fun, make a bunch of money, live cheaply, and that would be easy and fun.* I got rejection selling Typants; however, it was a drop in the bucket compared to what I got when I started out in mortgages. My boss at the time said, "Go out and work with real estate agents."

So, I went out and contacted as many real estate agents as I could. I had a lot of great conversations with them, but I didn't realize how many people were just blowing sunshine. They would meet with me and we would get along—and then nothing would happen. I would be so excited after a meeting—and nothing would happen. A week would pass, and then another week—and nothing, no business! During my first year, I think I worked harder than I ever had before. I never took a holiday, and I started work at eight in the morning and worked till eight at night, seven days a week. I was *incredibly* busy—or at least, I thought I was so busy. I didn't realize at the time (while I was chain-smoking) that I wasn't actually that busy at all; I was busy *thinking* about work, but not actually working.

I remember stewing over a deal that I had made a mistake on, thinking, *This will be the last mortgage I ever do. I'm going to end up back working at the pet food store I started at.* In hindsight, I just didn't know how to take action in the middle of a crisis. I had yet to learn how to compartmentalize. I believe that if, back then, I had counted up the hours I had spent actually doing something productive, it would have been in the neighbourhood of four to five hours per day. The good news is that in my first year, I doubled my income. I went from earning $32,500 to $65,000 that year! Even better news is that I actually kept more of money as well! As I had just purchased my house, and I worked ALL the time, at least I felt that way, I was able to use a lot of regular home expenses as tax deduction. I was able to reduce my PRE TAX income by over $25000 that year. I was much further ahead than when I was on a salary. This was a true reward for going commission, and I could see the potential of how much money I could not only make but save at the same time. I was even allowed to use some of the expenses from when I went out drinking with friends! AMAZING! A tax deduction for going out with my friends, what a beautiful country we live in! In fairness, all of my friends did get mortgages with me so we technically did talk business, for at least 5 or 10 minutes, "your approved, lets party!".

I was happy, but tired, as I knew there had to be a better way of doing things than how I was currently doing them. I was working so hard, and spending so much of my time thinking about work, even when I was not working. That was when I started to realize that I wasn't being present with people—my family included.

What I Made It Mean

I realized that I was on the right path, even though it felt like a tough choice and a ton of hard work, the tough work was resulting in much more money in my pocket. I started to really understand the value and the tax advantages in having your own business, or being commission based. This is also the time I decided it does not matter how much money people make. I used to always be so impressed when someone told me their income was $100,000 or $250,000 per year. I realized it was about how much money you keep at the end of the day. If you make $250,000 per year as an employee but the government tax is 45% of it, and then you pay your expenses, you would be better off making $180,000 of self employed income and keeping more of the money.

I understood that nothing comes easy; but by having great mentors in my business, and seeing their paycheques I decided this was the path for me to get to the top of the mountain. By going into a commission-based role, I could not make up excuses anymore if it wasn't working out for me. I chose to *make it work*. I learned that I had to continually work on my business and not give up. I also saw that most people in my industry last less than two years. This turns out to be true in most businesses and commission based roles. Unfortunately 90% of businesses will not succeed for more than 2 years. This was exciting to me, as it meant that if I stuck it out, I would have instant credibility just based on my longevity. I could do this; this was the one business that I had to stick with. The number-one guy in my company pulled in over $750,000 in commissions. I realized that I could do that too, but I would never be able to shoot for something like that if I had stayed in the branch and just tried to work harder in the corporate world. If I was to hit financial security by my Mission date, this would be how I was going to do it. I made a choice and said, "I am going to work this business, and it will pay off!"

What To Do

When you start up a business and you're having challenges, and it's not going the way that you anticipated, remember: this is normal! The important part is to not confuse your income goals with your learning goals. Even though I wasn't making the money I wanted to, I was learning tons of info about real estate, money, lending, and so on. Start a business, and if you do not know what to start, go on your social media and ask someone that you want to join a network marketing company and don't know which one to try. You will get hundreds of messages in a second I am quite sure. You will be surprised how many people are involved in these businesses but do not go out and promote it. They are shy and sometimes question as to weather or not they believe in what they are selling. That is why you need to find something you believe in, as if you have not even sold yourself on the idea, it will be damn hard to sell someone else on the idea as well. I tried network marketing and even though I did not make any money in the business, it definitely paved a great foundation for my learning and growth. Network marketing companies also have next to zero start up costs. There are not too many businesses that you can start, even part time that have no overhead, this can allow you to try multiple ones in order to find one that is in alignment with your passions.

If nothing else, it will give you the much needed tax deductions in order to save to invest more of your money. Even if the start up cost for the network marketing company is $500 and you make no money, this can be deducted against your employment income. I am positive you will get more out of it than the tax savings as you will meet so many amazing people with high hopes and goals for the future that it will prop you up as well.

Today, I am still learning new things about my industry that I find fascinating. Be a lifelong learner of your business when you find the one that you love; income will follow. When you start a business that you can work hard in *and* be rewarded in wheelbarrows full of money, don't forget that it will take time! If everyone got rich quick in your business right away, then everyone else would be doing it already. When you find a business and you love it, do not let the failure stop you. If there are people out there who are wildly more successful than you, then you know it is possible, so stick with it.

Chapter 8:
Reward Yourself
Along the Way

"Those who celebrate the small victories and
simple pleasures win the game over and over again."
—Unknown

Rewards can be a funny thing, as if you are like me you can put off rewarding yourself for sometime and almost punish yourself before giving into some gratification. Where as some people can be on the other end of the spectrum, where you feel like because you woke up this morning, you are entitled to a reward. There is balance that has to be drawn in the middle. As if you never reward yourself, then it is easy to lose track of what the Mission is all about. By having financial security, you should be able to have more fun in your life. Rewards along the way give you a taste of the things to come in your life, and can really motivate you! I remember taking my brother out for an exotic car day not too long ago, and we were able to rip around the race track in a Lamborghini Gallardo. Now that was a fun day! By having that little reward it reminded me of what I would like to continue to shoot for, and that money is meaningless until you put meaning on it. Not too mention that enjoying rewards with people you love is the best thing ever. I will never forget seeing his hands at 10 and 2 with a serious "Holy Shit" smile on his face.

Now if you are constantly rewarding yourself, you will look for bigger and better rewards, as the more you do, the more you need to be fulfilled. A reward is not truly juicy unless you have earned it. I love going on a vacation knowing that I worked my ass off. After putting in 12 hour days, back to back appointments, knowing I played full out, I an have a guilt free rest and enjoy. If you have not earned it, you will go away thinking about work, feeling guilty and what the heck is the point of that!

The trick is to ensure that you have your rewards laid out and at what milestones you are going to achieve them. Make sure that they spark some emotion in you as well, as if it doesn't make you jump out of bed the day you are going to collect them, you need to get more creative!

What Happened

I have definitely given myself wins along the way. I can think of three major rewards that meant a lot to me. The first one was purchasing my first single-family house that didn't have rental income attached to it. I was in my late twenties, I had four rental properties under my belt, and I purchased a fifth one to live in. It was a modest house, but it was completely finished. No renovations required, it was all done inside! I was tired of living in a place that was in constant need of renovations, and I realized that I wanted a place to come home to and actually relax. When I was in my duplex, I would come home to watch TV, fire up a premade pizza, have a homebrewed beer, and then look around at the house and say to myself, "Still gotta finish that, still gotta do that—and oh yeah, the deck is falling apart, I need to get that fixed. The kitchen still looks like shit, gotta do that. Jeez, so much to do!" I wasn't a handyman, but I was good with numbers, sales, and people, so in order to be my best self, I needed a place to call home that had nothing to do in it except for me to relax and focus on my tasks at hand.

My second big reward was when I purchased my first sports car. I had been saving for a couple years in my long-term savings for spending account. It was $30,000 at the time, which I had saved for over two years by putting a small amount of money away for each month. When I finally had enough, I bought my 2003 Nissan 350Z roadster. I loved that car—for about six months. It was so important to me to have a nice car; ever since I was a kid, I had thought it would be the coolest thing ever to have a fast car that was a convertible. I thought I was so cool driving that thing around—until one day, when I was cruising on the highway with the top down, it started to rain. I never went from thinking I was a hero to a zero quicker than that.

The third big reward for myself was when I purchased the house I am in today. It is an old Victorian building that is about 3,000 square feet on a 100- by 300-foot lot, nestled into the escarpment, where the entire backyard is full of trees. It truly is my sanctuary. As I write this now, on the patio by my pool, I really appreciate all the hard work and sacrifices that got me to this place. I was in my late twenties when I purchased it, and it has a rental suite in the basement, which helped me to pay it off quicker.

What I Made It Mean

Getting the car and the house meant to me that I was winning. It was so gratifying at the time to get those things, and I do not regret any of them one bit. However, I will say that I learned that joy does not come from having these possessions. The car didn't make me a better person, nor did it make me happier. The novelty soon wore off, and I actually was more worried about it when I drove it than I had thought I would be. It had such a low profile that I had to be careful not to bottom out when going up and down driveways. I even sometimes felt a little embarrassed by it when I would show up at the houses of clients who were in a less fortunate position financially than me. The happiness the car brought me was temporary, in that I learned that there are more important things than the car you drive.

To be truthful, I actually got more satisfaction in my head when I was driving my Ford Escape in my early thirties, knowing that I was on my way to Mission 35. It brought me more joy knowing that I wasn't a slave to my possession. I would drive that truck, and if it got dinged in the parking lot by a shopping cart, or if some careless asshole backed into me and scratched the bumper, I would think to myself, *Oh well! No worries—it still runs, it's in good shape, and no one will consider stealing it.*

Getting my first house made me understand the value of the hard work and having my own sanctuary to call home. In my eyes, it is important to have a peaceful place to come home to—a place where you feel safe, secure, and at ease. If you are worried about paying the bills because the mortgage is too high, or if you're stressed that the roof needs to be replaced because you are living paycheque to paycheque, it's not worth it! Living within my means has always given me more gratification than the fleeting compliments received by having a nice car or a nice house.

The house that I live in today, was my dream home, but it didn't start that way. It was the dream lot, and the dream bones, we had to renovate almost every room in it, which we did over the course of 5 years. I remember drinking a bottle (or 3) of wine with my wife one night tearing off 4 layers of wall paper only to find more wall paper. That was a real bonding experience, which I don't recommend for any newlyweds. Those renovations were hard, but being in the house that I knew I would raise a family in, made it fun for us. My house didn't come with a pool; I actually sold my sports car in order to put the pool in! It didn't nearly cover the $100,000 landscaping job for the pool, hot tub, two-tier deck, elaborate stone patio, and tiki bar (I love that tiki bar)! But in selling the car, I thought to myself, *You can only have one toy right now. The backyard is going to be your luxury, not the car—not until you achieve your Mission of financial security.* I have to say the true reward of buying, renovating and putting in the pool on the house was the people that we have shared it with over the years. Growing up, my parents were extremely gracious hosts, and I always wanted to be the same way. My wife and I would throw epic parties, with lights, bartenders, fire eaters, and even a DJ on the balcony. I remember one in particular where I even ended up snow blowing my driveway at 2am, in the middle of August. This was a great way to get to know the neighbors! To this day we still host Christmas and many of the family events, and it brings me so much joy to see other people enjoy the rewards that we have worked so hard for. As it turns out one of the secrets to living is giving.

The house, which may seem like a large indulgence, was a practical choice too. Both my wife and I like to travel, but we also were working a lot (as we were in commission sales), and our weekends were often quite busy. We were different from many other people in their early thirties, who, when they start to accumulate bigger incomes and paying off debt, end up getting second homes, such as a cottage, ski chalet, or even a trailer. The decision to make our backyard our secondary home was an obvious winner. The upfront cost came from the sale of one of my rental properties, and the backyard can be enjoyed on a daily basis, rather than for just a couple weeks out of the year.

What To Do

Celebrate your wins! If you do not do this, you will lose sight of your achievements and goals, and depending on your age, it can be a *long* time to wait to give yourself some gratification.

Pick three milestone rewards that you will have to save for, and plan when you want to get them. These rewards must be within your reality (see Mission 35's website, under "Rewards") and be based on your income. Next, arrange your budget. Put a percentage of your income away in order to purchase your rewards in cash. However, if it is a house you are looking to purchase on your Mission, ensure that you have at least a 20% down payment for it from savings, and have a plan in place to get it paid off by the end of your Mission.

A car, for example, is not a reward if it is financed or leased. You may be thinking that you need a *fancy* car in order to do well in commission sales, but I call bullshit! I know many people in different industries who were able to drive a reasonable car and make *lots* of money.

Do not put off your planned indulgent purchases, because as I have mentioned, you need to experience the fleeting gratification for yourself. It will help you make smarter decisions as you go along your journey, and it will also help you to think twice about doing something *really* stupid when you have millions to spend. The more money you have, the more problems you can get into, so make sure you reward yourself with some amazing things along the way. Sometimes, the reward you so desperately wanted comes, and then you learn an even more valuable lesson about your own self-awareness; however, you have to experience it to get it.

Chapter 9:
Focus Your Efforts

Focusing your efforts leads to mastery.

*"If people knew how hard I worked to get my mastery,
it wouldn't seem so wonderful at all."*
—Michelangelo

The goal is to become the master at what you focus your efforts on. Once you discover what your part time passion business is, or what your full-time business is going to be, you need to weed out all the other distractions. This is where you will really start to multiply your earnings! Keep learning it, but learn it like no one else. Again, as I said earlier, do not be the person who has 1 year experience ten times. Keep learning about your craft as if it were your first year every year. Keep seeking out mentors for your business and find out how you can be the absolute best at it. I have met many people who are well into their thirties that have tried so many different commission-based jobs or network marketing companies, and they always have an excuse for why it didn't work out—or there was someone in the organization who was keeping them down.

Bullshit! It will be hard! Anything that is of value does not come easy. When things get hard—and especially if it is something that you love—do not quit. Do not give up. Find help, and find a way to overcome the obstacles. Once you do, your focus will become like a ninja's, and you will become better than you could imagine. As time goes on, your friends and co-workers will identify you as someone with great leadership skills, commitment, and integrity—all of which are amazing traits! However, what will also come with this is a *number* of different opportunities to get involved in. The "shiny balls" as we say. The trick is to ensure that you stay focused on the plan, do not deviate and chase the shiny balls, stay focused on the mission.

What Happened

When I was in my late twenties and my investable assets started to climb, there was the temptation to get involved more heavily in trading stocks. I had seen a number of clients and even friends make good money out of buying and selling. I had toyed many times with the thought of opening up a discount brokerage stock trading account and learning day trading to make my investments grow rapidly. Or by buying the latest stock tip that a friend of a friend of a friend told me about to make a huge gain. I have also been offered to invest in different businesses that I knew little to nothing about.

I tried my hand at flipping properties; this was an endeavour that I still believe I made little to no money at. I had two full-time contractors on payroll, and through my knowledge of the mortgage market, I devised a plan to purchase, fix, refinance, and rent out the units. The thought was that I could invest a certain amount of money and then get it all back through the refinance, and have cashflow left over. This two years of my life was again very busy, with not only monitoring and being on top of my commission-based business, but also being on top of the renovations, the costs going out the door, and the timelines in order to ensure that our goals were being met. Nothing pissed me off more than stopping by unannounced to one of the projects and seeing my contractors sitting on their asses playing cards while I was paying them. Don't be that guy!

With that being said, I still thought it was a very *cool* thing to be doing. We would find terrible houses that needed work, and I could see them transform into something beautiful. I really did love seeing that transition. I would even help out to get the work done quicker by going in at five in the morning to do the painting. That was about the extent of my handy work (which my wife has now fired me from doing in our own home). My impatience tells me that I can get a room painted in less than a day, so my edging and lack of preparation makes for a painting job that looks like a blind guy did it (no staying in the lines here!). But if you want me to just roll the paint on anywhere, I am your guy! Even though flipping homes gave me excitement and I liked seeing the transformation of things this was truly a "shiny ball" for me. I was more caught up in how "cool" I thought it was than actually looking at the numbers to see if it made financial sense.

When I truly focused on my mortgage business, I was at the top of my game as a commission-based mortgage person, and I needed to transition into having an actual business. This required completely different skills than what had made me successful as a mortgage person. I was actually on a quest to find who was the best in the business and why. I was fortunate enough to go on many top performers trips (for free, I might add, which is another *huge* benefit of focusing and getting to be the best at your business), and instead of partying my face off on another company's dime, I would go around and talk to everyone I could and ask them questions about how they conducted their business. When you are networking with high producers, they usually have *no problem* at all with telling you why they are so great and what they did to become so great. I found out that there were very few people in my industry who had actually transitioned from being a commission-based person to a business owner. If they left the business, the business was done.

I then expanded my search outside of Canada to find out how other people in the world were conducting their businesses in the same industry as mine. I ended up at a Mortgage Expo in Las Vegas (not a bad time learning there, I might add). I ended up finding a coach there who helped me get into a mindset and gave me tools to see another way of doing things. Today, I am actually at a point where I can leave for a month and *still* have income from my business come in, as if I never left. What a good feeling this is!

What I Made It Mean

I had to stay focused on what made me money. By spending time on the flips, my commission-based business didn't grow, and it even started to dwindle a bit. I realized that it is important to perfect the things that you are good at, and not think you are the best at something, so you can in fact be the best at everything! I learned that the investments that made me the most money were the ones I hadn't changed much over the years; I just kept them for a long time. Buying and holding real estate for me has yielded the best returns out of my investment portfolio. It turns out that Warren Buffet, with his buy-and-hold strategy, was on to something! He's not one of the richest men in the world for nothing.

I was under the illusion that because I had made a decent amount of money doing what I was doing that I could do anything really well (I was a bit delusional, to say the least). This is a common god-like complex that we need to be careful of when we start to get a little bit of success. "Everything I touch turns to gold!" Not bloody likely.

When I really started to focus on my mortgage business, and I left the bank to go out on my own when I was thirty-two years old, things blew up. I didn't buy any more rentals, flip any houses, or try to trade stocks; I just focused on transitioning my commission-based business into a *real* business. This was one of the hardest things to do, and it took all of my efforts; instead of spreading myself over two to three different investments, I focused *all* of my efforts on my mortgage business. I was spending over eighty hours a week on learning, mentors, clients, applications, payroll, and training, and I was trying to learn everything I could to get me to the next level. At no point would I even entertain something different, as I was so laser-focused on my one business and making it grow.

When I got to my second year in my own business, I was able to *save* $250,000. That is a number that, as I have grown, is much more important than the money I made. Being able to save $250,000 in one year—after *all* of my expenses—was huge! This was something that catapulted me and my FIA number at thirty-three years old. At the beginning of the book, when I mentioned how your FIA number can be daunting, it has a compound effect. Picture the skyscraper: If you have seen one going up, it seems like the construction workers are working in the ground for eternity, sometimes for up to two years. Then, all of a sudden, you see twenty stories go up in three months. This is all about taking the time to lay an incredible foundation for growth. In the last two years of my Mission 35, my asset base grew by over $600,000. This wasn't a coincidence; this was all due to my timing, hard work, and effort. When you truly focus on being a master at your business, this can happen for you, as well.

What To Do

Find out what you love, and stick with it. If you think you have, then make it to the top of your game. Than stick with it, and try to do even better. Who is going to stop you from redefining your business all together? There is always more to learn in the industry you are in, which means there is also always more money to be made. Find the absolute best coaches in your industry and hire them. What got you to this point was consistency and hard work. As I said before, there is no secret sauce; you just need to work harder and harder at every stage of the game you are playing, stay focused and with it will be more rewards.

The big "*however!*" is this: If you do find yourself making the same amount of money or more in your second investment, then by all means, continue to pursue it. Mission 35 does mean multiple income streams and multiple positions at the same time. I eventually bought my own office (my first commercial property) and a second one 5 years later. This was still consistent with my real estate investment philosophy of buying a rental with positive cash flow. I thought what better tenant than myself to pay rent, not too mention that each property had a residential unit with it as well to subsidize my costs. This also created a huge tax savings for me as I was able to have one corporation that I owned (my mortgage business) pay rent to another corporation I owned (my real estate company). As your corporate tax rate is currently less than 20% of your income if you move money from one company to another without taking the income personally (as it is taxed higher) you can buy more real estate with funds that are taxed at a lower rate. Once you get into the higher tax brackets making over $150,000 per year, you are saving almost 20 cents on every dollar! Put this into perspective, when you are laser focused business starts to thrive, and you are staying within your budgets, you can save lots of money. If you are making $250,000 per year and you can live off of say $100,000 per year, that would be $100,000 you can use to purchase more property. This is almost a $50,000 savings of money you get to keep and invest back into yourself! I believe if you are in a business that requires a retail or office space, make sure you do all you can to OWN the real estate. By becoming the owner you are paying yourself twice, once through your business and again through the rent you can charge yourself. By staying focused on my strengths in business and not overly diversifying I have been able to grow my asset base exponentially. How do you feel about diversity now?

Be cautious as to what you are investing in, and be sure not to spread yourself thin, but also be realistic with the amount of time that is in a week. Remember how many hours it took you to be a rock star at what you are currently doing. It will most likely take you the same amount of invested time to do almost anything. Malcolm Gladwell coined the "10,000-hour rule" which states that when you have invested 10,000 hours in one subject or area, you become a certified professional at it. For most people, based on a fifty-hour time investment per week, this equates to just under four years at fifty-two weeks a year, with no vacations.

Check out our Mission 35 website to see possible options that would line up with your interests. Stay focused on the Mission, the results will compound before you know it.

Chapter 10:
Giving Back Keeps You Grounded

"The meaning of life is to find your gift.
The purpose of life is to give it away."
—*Pablo Picasso*

There are a ton of ways that you can contribute to your community or give back to society. There is something about contributing and giving to others that deeply satisfies you more than any paycheque will. When people would tell me this in the past, I would usually shake my head and say to myself, sure thing I'll give when I have enough for myself. There is something cosmic that happens, when you let go, you actually get more. Its like the monkey trap. In the jungle in order to trap a monkey they will put food in a small whole in the tree, when the monkey grabs the food and tries to get it out, it will never let go! This is the equivalent to living in a scarcity mentality instead of an abundance mentality. There are so many things you can do in order to give back. You can volunteer at a hospital, soup kitchen, inner city school, big brothers and big sisters, the SPCA or a hospice. You can even spend an afternoon picking up garbage in a nearby park. There is no shortage of options to volunteer your time making our world a better place. I fully understand this could be the last thing you are interested in doing when you are chasing the mighty dollar! The alternative is becoming a money-hungry monster that forgets about all of mankind, and I have come across a lot of these people, as I am sure you have. I had a sales officer in a previous mortgage company who insisted on telling everyone how much his net worth was growing all the time, and even though he was quite successful, everyone would loathe talking to him. The more he got, the more friends he lost. Giving back is not just about money; it is easy to give money when you have a ton of it, but if you don't, make the best use of your time! Take away one hour a week of your social media time and you will be a better person for it, I promise—so long as you are donating your time to someone or something else. You do have time for this, no matter what your circumstances are, and it will add to your life—not take from it. When you have a bad day and you do something for someone else who is less fortunate, it puts your problems and issues into perspective. I was at a sales conference and the speaker said, "I guarantee that if we were able to put all of your problems into a box up front here, and you could come pick out someone else's problem and take it home instead of your own, you would all be begging for your own problems back by the time you go to your car!" Giving back wither your time or your money will teach your brain that no matter what you have, or give away you can always get it back. By not doing this you are re enforcing a negative trait that you have to hold on to everything.

What Happened

I returned home after travelling to Australia for university and then touring through South East Asia for two months (specifically in Bangkok, Vietnam, and Cambodia). I had some very eye-opening experiences; as you can imagine, I had been backpacking and not staying at any of the Hiltons along the way—not even a Motel 6 was in my budget when I was travelling. I had an overwhelming need to sell some pants, *and* to give back somehow. I realized how absolutely amazing and fortunate we are to be in a developed country where just about anything is possible if you have the right mindset, motivation, and ideas.

It was at this time that I signed up to be a Big Brother. I didn't have any money to contribute to a good cause, so the best thing I could do was donate my time. I got linked up with an amazing kid named Alex. It first started with me being an in-school mentor. I would go to his school and spend an hour a week with him, playing games, making cookies, or whatever else to pass the time. When I met some of Alex's friends, it hit home for me to realize how lucky I was to have two amazing parents who had given me such a good foundation of values. I remember asking one of Alex's girl friends what she wanted to do when she grew up. She looked at me with a beautiful smile and all sincerity and said, "I want to be just like my mom when I grow up!"

I said, "That's awesome. What does she do?"

The little girl let out an eager and excited laugh and said, "She collects a cheque every month and goes shopping!"

Wow, my heart sank. This is what happens and what kids see when their parents are on a fixed income or social assistance. That was her dream; that was what she was shooting and striving for in life. This made me realize that there needs to be more people out there trying to help communicate to kids—especially those who don't come from the best of families—that there is more to life. School teachers, for the most part, do an amazing job of this! (I say "for the most part" as there are teachers out there who are just punching the clock.) But even they cannot be everyone's role model every day; they already have a full schedule!

Big Brother was an amazing opportunity to try and make a small difference with one person. As time went by, I got to see Alex on the weekends and take him to the movies, out for lunch, and to the beach. This small amount of time (two to four hours on a weekend) allowed me to stay grounded with what I was trying to achieve, and it really put some much-needed perspective in my life.

What I Made It Mean

Being a Big Brother was important to me, in that when I was so focused on making money, it still made me feel like a human being. It also gave me motivation to keep going, as with more money you have more opportunities to make a difference. Being able to accomplish my Mission has allowed me the space in my life to go on this new journey of giving back by showing people that there is another way to live their lives. This has become my new vision on how I can help (and hopefully inspire) people to live differently. In a world where materialism is rewarded, I think it is more important than ever to communicate that there is *more* to life. There is *more* to give if you focus your time and efforts on the right things. I also learned that there is more joy in giving back than there is in living a completely selfish life. If you haven't experienced this already you will, it is actually a fundamental human need to give back in a way that is greater than yourself. I had heard about this through many conferences, CDs, and speakers that I had listened to over the years, and really tried to find out what I would do. Only by fulfilling my need for financial security (hitting my FIA number) was I able to truly find my calling for elevating peoples financial literacy. This is a goal that will never be completed and helps to keep my life full.

The monetary gain from giving back can sometimes be seen, and sometimes it cannot. If you are in business, having a cause that you give to (or one that you are passionate about) will also put you into a different network of people who have similar goals and values as you. People like to do business with people who have the same values in life. Because my dad passed away from cancer, our company did numerous fundraisers for the hospital where he had stayed. I was able to really connect with a lot of the amazing nurses and staff who helped him out. As a result, we were able to do business together, as well. However, I will caution you super-ambitious souls out there who *only* volunteer or join a charity to get business: I do not believe this works, as it will come across as disingenuous and insincere. Only when you are truly giving to give will the business come as a result. Find something that sticks for you and means something. You will get so much more out of it.

What To Do

I think this is a no-brainer, but I will spell it out: Go volunteer somewhere, anywhere! Do something that means something to you, and I guarantee that it will not only give you perspective, but it will also fill you full of joy and give you tons of energy. Doing charity work or running a fundraiser puts a whole new spin on your Mission journey. It will expand your mind, your thinking, and introduce you to some truly amazing people. Our Mission 35 Education Program has some great volunteer ideas.

You do not have to have money to give back. People will typically have two things to give: time or money (or both). When you are starting out on your Mission, you will most likely have the time and not the money, so use it. As you progress and your resources grow, give some back! I love being able to sponsor my customers and co-workers' hockey teams, as it reminds me of when I played, and how much my dad had to kick in from his paycheque so that both me and my brother could play.

Google different charities and organizations in your area, and try them out. If you don't like it, you don't have to stay with it; you can try another one. Just because you try one and don't like it doesn't make you a bad person. Also, try mixing this charity work with your social time; do it with your boyfriend, spouse, or a group of friends. The more fun you make it, the bigger contribution you will make, which will also have the biggest impact.

Chapter 11:
Attitude:
Pick A Good One

*"You will never reach your destination if you stop
and throw stones at every dog that barks."*
—*Winston Churchill.*

Fulfillment is all about how you look at life. Is it bogging you down, or is it making you smile? Do you have huge problems, or do you have some unique challenges? It's all in how you frame it in your mind, and it stems from your attitude. What you consistently think about and how you think about it will be a huge determining factor in your success at whatever you do. People want to associate with positive people. Let me correct that—*you* want to associate with positive people. I'm not talking about pot-smoking hippies here who think everything is just *great*; I'm talking about people who legitimately believe in you—people who have dreams and are not afraid to voice them and try to reach for them.

What Happened

When I was young, I played a lot of competitive hockey. I remember my first tryouts when I was younger; I was trying out for the AA team. I had always been what I thought was an okay player—I wasn't the best, but definitely not the worst. I was so nervous and excited about trying out for this team, as it would mean I was kind of a big deal if I made it (mind you, it was a big deal for me at the age of twelve, whoopee!). But nonetheless, I was nervous. The tryouts were gruelling, and I thought I was a long shot, but I ended up making the team. I wasn't totally surprised, as my dad was whispering in my ear that he thought I had a really good shot (positive Pete)—and again, I wasn't the worst one out there.

The big surprise came when we were three exhibition games in, and it was time to pick a team captain. I was sitting in the dressing room all suited up and ready to go. Coach Jack was giving his pre-game speech, and he looked over at me, pointed, and said, "There's your team captain." *What the hell!* I thought. I was looking around, and there were so many guys that I thought were *way* better than me—and way cooler, too. I was in shock! I actually thought Jack was pointing to the guy next to me, but then I slowly realized he was looking and pointing at *me*. He said, "We need someone on this team who is not only a team player, but who demonstrates the attitude of what we want our team to be. Never give up, and always try your best." I guess I was Rudy! This was one of those moments in life that stuck out for me. I was so scared, yet also so up for the responsibility, as well. Not to mention, I thought it would go well with the girls I knew at the time to say I was the captain of the hockey team.

What the coach saw in me, which I hadn't realized yet, was my attitude. I was always encouraging the other players on the team, and I was always looking at how we could do better. I used to get the "most sportsmanlike player" award all the time, and some of my friends would affectionately refer to it as the "pansy award." This was because the sportsman like player usually also had the least amount of penalty minutes. (Thanks, guys!) Seriously, though—the award and the compliment of being the team captain weren't based on my skills (as much as I wanted them to be); they were totally based on my attitude. Thanks, Dad.

What I Made It Mean

Being rewarded and ridiculed all at the same time for receiving the "most sportsmanlike" award gave me some conflicting thoughts for a while. As I was not sure what I should be valuing more. On one hand I did not want to be a pansy, but on the other hand I valued the respect I had for being a team player. Reflecting back on it, being the "most sportsman-like" and being team captain for several years gave me the confidence I needed to see myself as someone who others respected and believed in for leadership. It gave me the confidence to be who I wanted to be, and to not cower to others' beliefs about what I should be, or who I should be. I truly appreciated this opportunity, as it had come from my father, through and through. He is gone now, but I find myself having "Dad moments." Moments where I feel like I am channeling his attitude and thoughts into a situation. My dad truly had the best attitude of any person I have ever met. He would be the guy who could sneak up on someone and point out something good about them (when so many of us do the opposite). His positive attitude truly gave me the foundation I needed at a young age—even though I didn't realize it—and this would help me to excel in my personal relationships throughout my life; it would also help me to always see the good. As I think back on it today, he never actually said this to me in words, which just goes to show how actions speak louder than words (as we have all heard before). I didn't know how important attitude was when I was young, playing hockey and other sports (I suppose I was unconsciously aware); however, when growing my commission-based mortgage business, I was acutely aware of how to handle myself in my personal relationships.

What To Do

Surround yourself with people who believe in you, and who support you. We all know the ones who will say, "yeah right, buddy," and try to beat you down at every curve.

I had a very good friend, who I met in grade 9 through other mutual friends and instantly hit it off. I think it was because we were both huge loud mouths in high school. He was one of my best friends, and he was even the best man at my wedding. We had so much in common; we were both mortgage brokers, active Big Brothers, we both owned rental proper-ties, and we both loved to party! The one thing we didn't have in common was our attitude. He would use drugs and alcohol to escape his feelings, where as I was the happy drunk all the time. I would take a hard look at yourself and see what partying does for you, I know for sure that it takes away focus from what I am doing, and I actually have more fun now being sober. Who would have thought?! I am not saying that you have to give up these vices if you have them, but truly look at what kind of person it makes you, what are you gaining, and what it is costing you, financially and emotionally. My friend was the life of the party when he was drinking, and I had so much fun with him, but he could turn at any moment (especially the next day or 2) and look at the negative of what was wrong in any situation, then resort to playing the victim. Our friendship eventually ended after he had partied his body into the emergency room from alcohol and drugs, and my wife and I rushed to his side while he was on death's door. He was on life support for several weeks, and I would visit him as much as possible. I had never seen someone with that many tubes and machines hooked up to their body at one time. I knew it was serious, but for some reason, it didn't compute—because after all, we were in our early thirties, and we were still "invincible"! While he made some very poor life choices, I believe that had he changed his attitude on things, he would not have needed all the distractions that partying gives you, and he would have been able to see all the amazing things that were happening for him. Instead, the negativity contributed to a downward spiral that changed his life forever. Even after this I would have thought that his attitude would have changed, having a new lease on life and all, but it didn't, he was even more resentful than ever before.

Having a positive attitude will bring you more good fortune than anything else you can do. I never was the smartest person, the funniest, the best-looking (unless you asked my mom), or the most business-savvy guy; however, I always had a positive attitude when it came to situations. Some people would accuse me of being a pushover, because I would not get mad—nor get even—whenever someone was disloyal or did something that deserved severe negative repercussions. My belief is that holding bitterness and revenge is like drinking poison and expecting the other person to die (I know I read this somewhere in my travels). The other person does not give a shit about you, so why bother putting all that negative energy into something that is completely unproductive? I believe that I have gained—as will you—a *tremendous* amount of respect by choosing this path. Have I stumbled along the way? Absolutely, but I would say this has happened after I have been around negative people for a period of time, and when I haven't been of healthy body and mind. Attitude can and will be affected by drugs and alcohol—*no shit, eh?* Seriously though, I am not even talking about when you are drunk or high, but when your sober the next day—it is twice as hard to get your body and mind back to the positive state. If you have ever woken up with a depressed or guilty feeling from what happened the night before, then you know what I am talking about, and if you haven't, then *don't!* You're not missing anything. I would tell people (and I still do today) that I don't get hangovers, which was an outright lie. The truth was that, after a long night of drinking and partying with friends, I knew that I had to work twice as hard as anyone else the next day in order to achieve my Mission; so, I would get up at the crack of dawn (not shortly after I had gone to bed some nights) and start running. I would go for a run, sometimes still buzzed, to sweat it out of my system, and to convince everyone else (but especially myself) that I didn't get hangovers. This allowed me to remain focused on the task at hand, and on my positive attitude, even after a night of being a blithering idiot.

I have to admit that it is getting a bit harder to do this, so I play a little game on the rare occasions that I want to go out and relive my youth. I will drive to the location of the party, bar, or friend's house where we will be drinking and leave my car there. I then have to run there in the morning in order to get my car. (It's a good thing that most of my outings are within 5 km of the house!) Your attitude is everything, and it will be the one thing that keeps you going on your Mission.

In Closing

Every day, you have choices. The tougher ones you make, the more you start to create your path. One big choice I made when I was younger was to stop playing hockey. I was the captain of the team for two years in a row, and I was a very good player at my age. (Several of the people that I played with went on to do a great job in the NHL.) I got to an age where I decided that I wanted to be a rock star and play in a band instead of being a hockey player. (Wow—I should have looked at the league's minimum salary at the time, which was approximately $300,000 per year. I could have been writing *Mission 25* or *Mission 30* if I had have stayed! Okay, maybe this is a bad example.)

The good news is that choices get easier as you get used to making tougher ones. It is hard when you are young and single, and especially when you start making some money. Do I go on a cool trip, make a down payment on a *very* cool car, or do I invest it in my first piece of real estate? Do I buy a house that lots of girls will think, "Hello," or do I buy a house that will allow me to say "Goodbye" to working a job because I have to? The beauty of these choices is the compounding of it; as it gets easier, the more confidence you will get. I would often times feel more confident the less I had. Just before my thirty-third birthday, when I was pulling in over half a million dollars a year and rolling around in my old Ford Escape. People just didn't know what to think, but I knew who I was and what I was, and it felt good rolling up to a stop light, and even when there was a *way* nicer car beside me, I thought to myself, *This bitch is paid for, and then some!* You really don't need to prove anything to anyone, except for yourself. Sell yourself on your Mission and the rest will take care of itself.

All of the chapters in this book will help you keep your spirits up, which will keep you on a positive note. You will get tired, frustrated, pissed off, and want to quit, and that is totally normal. When this does happen, remember to look at what you have accomplished so far; look at your goals and the ones you have achieved, and look at where you are going and the freedom you will have. You will be the envy of all your friends and family, because it will take hard work, and it won't be easy. Being able to accelerate your retirement is something that will make the rest of your life a new beginning. You will have your *entire* life ahead of you to make choices because you want to, *not* because you have to. You will be able to spend more time with your family, with your kids when you have them, and with all of your loved ones. You will be a beacon of what life should be like for people. Be the example of how to live in a world where people are not burnt-out and frustrated, too tired to speak, or too overworked and overwhelmed to answer a simple question or say "Hi" to a stranger on the street—I dare you to do it. I know you can, and I truly hope that you do. This is my way of trying to help you along the way.

Good luck on you Mission!

Printed in Canada